SCM STUDYGUIDE
TO NEW TESTAMENT
INTERPRETATION

Ian Boxall

scm press

British Library Cataloguing in Publication data

A catalogue record for this book is available
from the British Library

978 0 334 04048 4

First published in 2007 by SCM Press
St Mary's Works, St Mary's Plain,
Norwich, Norfolk, NR3 3BH

www.scm-canterburypress.co.uk

SCM Press is a division of
SCM-Canterbury Press Ltd

Typeset by Regent Typesetting, London
Printed and bound in Great Britain by
Creative Print and Design, Wales

Contents

Acknowledgements

This book, and its companion volume *SCM Studyguide to the Books of the New Testament*, are the fruit of teaching and learning from generations of ordinands and undergraduates, first at Chichester Theological College, and subsequently at St Stephen's House, Oxford, and within the wider University of Oxford. I am thankful to them for their part in making New Testament study such an exciting enterprise, and to colleagues at both colleges for their support and insight. Thanks also are due to Barbara Laing and her staff at SCM Press for their assistance and encouragement.

My sister Nicola died suddenly while I was in the process of writing this book. It is dedicated to her memory in love, and in gratitude for the ongoing love and support of my brother-in-law Robin and my nephew Michael.

In memory of a much-loved sister
Nicola Christine Johnson
1963–2006

and with love and gratitude
to Robin and Michael

Introduction

Purpose of this Book

The purpose of this studyguide is plainly and simply to encourage you to read and interpret the New Testament, and to open up the rich variety of ways in which it can be studied and the range of questions it raises. Ideally, it is aimed to be used in conjunction with the *SCM Studyguide to the Books of the New Testament*, which deals with the New Testament writings more systematically and in more detail. Nevertheless, each volume is sufficiently self-contained to be usable in its own right.

Chapter 1 is an orientation chapter, raising initial questions about the New Testament, and plotting the landscape of New Testament scholarship. Subsequent chapters aim to build on one another as they introduce different approaches to New Testament interpretation. New Testament scholarship is now so diverse that what is covered will inevitably reflect particular interests and knowledge, but an attempt has been made to provide as broad a range as is possible within a manageable compass. Most chapters conclude with a short list of suggestions for 'Further Reading'. Those wishing to pursue particular issues in more detail should also refer to books and articles mentioned in the endnotes.

Throughout the studyguide, there are questions for 'reflection', or more practical 'tasks' to help you put into practice what has been learnt. Some of these may be done individually, others are better done as shared exercises. Given that interaction is by far the best pedagogic method, they are an integral part of the book and should not be ignored. They are aimed at getting you interpreting the New Testament yourself as quickly and confidently as possible. At the end of this volume, there is a 'Putting it into Practice' section, which offers a worked example of a particular New Testament passage.

'Tool Kit' for New Testament Study

The following are useful resources for the student of the New Testament:

- A good **English Study Bible**, with introductions and notes (for further information on different English translations, see Chapter 4)
- A **Greek New Testament**: either the United Bible Societies' *Greek New Testament* or the Nestle-Aland *Novum Testamentum Graece*.
- A **Synopsis of the Gospels** (setting out parallel accounts in the different gospels side-by-side; some just covering the synoptic gospels, some all four). Two good versions are: Kurt Aland, 1982, *Synopsis of the Four Gospels*, United Bible Societies; B. H. Throckmorton, *Gospel Parallels*, Nashville: Thomas Nelson, various editions.
- A **concordance**: there are a number based on different English translations; on the Greek text, W. F. Moulton and H. K. Geden, 1963, *A Concordance to the Greek Testament*, Edinburgh: T. & T. Clark.
- A good **Bible atlas**: two useful examples are Yohanan Aharoni, Michael Avi-Yonah, Anson F. Rainey and Ze'ev Safrai (eds), 1993, *The Macmillan Bible Atlas*, 3rd edition, New York: Macmillan; Herbert G. May (ed., 3rd edition revised by John Day), 1984, *The Oxford Bible Atlas*, Oxford, New York and Toronto: Oxford University Press.
- A good **New Testament introduction**: among the most accessible, to keep on the shelf and use for reference, are: Raymond E. Brown, 1997, *An Introduction to the New Testament*, New York and London: Doubleday; Luke Timothy Johnson, 1999, *The Writings of the New Testament: An Interpretation*, revised edition; London: SCM Press.
- Scholarly **commentaries**: there are two one-volume commentaries to the whole Bible which are especially valuable to students: Raymond E. Brown, Joseph A. Fitzmyer and Roland E. Murphy (eds), 1995, *The New Jerome Bible Commentary*, London: Geoffrey Chapman; John Barton and John

Muddiman (eds), 2001, *The Oxford Bible Commentary*, Oxford: Oxford University Press. There are a large number of commentary series and stand-alone commentaries covering New Testament books: among these, series of particular note are the Anchor Bible, Black's New Testament Commentaries, Sacra Pagina and Word Commentaries.

- For the serious student, **Bible software** is a valuable aid: one of the best packages for Windows-based computers is *Bibleworks* (for up-to-date information, see www.bibleworks.com). A good package for Mac users is *Accordance* (www.accordancebible.com).
- There are huge numbers of **web resources** relating to the New Testament, of variable quality. One of the best, with links to large numbers of other scholarly websites, is Mark Goodacre's *New Testament Gateway* (www.nt gateway.com).

1

Introducing the New Testament

What is the New Testament?

Imagine that you are the manager of a large bookshop, who has never encountered the New Testament before. A supply of books entitled 'the New Testament' arrive for cataloguing and shelving. How are you going to categorize this new and intriguing book? Where are you going to place it on the shelves? What kind of book is it? Consulting Christian friends, or doing an internet search, might help. However, even this will probably throw up a range of possible answers to and perspectives on your question.

The simplest answer is probably this: the New Testament is a collection of 27 early Christian writings. These writings are quite diverse, including what look like four 'lives of Jesus', a 'history' of the early Church, a series of letters attributed to important early Christian leaders, possibly an early sermon or two, and a book full of rather disturbing visions. They also vary considerably in length (in an English study version I possess, from less than 1 page to approximately 50 pages).

But calling these diverse books 'the New Testament' (rather than 'the new testaments') is to talk of them as a coherent entity. Indeed, they are often bound together in a separate volume (so that the phrase 'New Testament' can be used to describe the object on the shelf), or printed as the shorter part of a more substantial volume entitled 'The Bible' or 'The Holy Bible'. In other words, 'the New Testament' appears to be not simply a disparate collection of 27 books, but 1 book, or Volume 2 of a much larger work (the Bible, comprising 'Old' and 'New' Testaments). The relationship between the parts and the whole, as we shall see, continues to be one of the most hotly debated issues in New Testament scholarship. How much weight should one give to individual voices within the New Testament? Can one detect a single overarching message, or a uniting voice, permeating the whole? Or is it rather a cacophony of competing voices?

Furthermore, to speak of 'the New Testament' at all is to make a religious claim for these writings. It is possible to study these 27 books as inspirational literature (alongside say Shakespeare or the poetry of Wordsworth), or as first-century examples of *koine* Greek (the 'common' Greek widely spoken in the Roman world), or in order to learn about the historical emergence of Christianity. All are involved in New Testament scholarship, and are to be encouraged. But to call these 27 writings 'the New Testament' (as opposed to 'early Christian writings') is to set them apart from other early Christian literature, and to connect them with 'the Old Testament', the sacred writings shared with Jews. It marks them off from, say, the apocryphal *Gospel of Thomas*, the letters of Ignatius of Antioch or the recently published *Gospel of Judas Iscariot*, as a group of writings regarded as in some sense foundational by the Christian churches. Foundational, that is, because the Christian community has recognized a certain authority in them, as the earliest authoritative witnesses to God's action in Jesus Christ. For Christians, these are not simply ancient texts, dead letters, but texts which convey the living word.

Different Things to Different People

There is a further, less evident reason why talking about the New Testament is not quite so simple. It has looked rather different and meant rather different things to different generations of Christians. If you visit the biblical manuscript displays at the British Library in London, you will see a diverse collection of New Testaments, or excerpts from the New Testament. Some are printed, but many are handwritten. Some are beautifully illuminated and obviously very costly. Some are large and very heavy, and not designed for use by ordinary people. Some are in English (though not necessarily

---

Table 1: The Books of the New Testament.

Gospels
Matthew
Mark
Luke
John

Acts
The Acts of the Apostles

Letters
Paul's Letters to Communities (Romans, 1 and 2 Corinthians, Galatians, Ephesians, Philippians, Colossians, 1 and 2 Thessalonians)
Paul's Letters to Individuals (1 and 2 Timothy, Titus [the 'Pastoral Epistles']; Philemon)
Hebrews (homily rather than letter?)
Catholic Epistles (James, 1 and 2 Peter, 1, 2 and 3 John, Jude)

Apocalypse
Revelation

---

easily readable to modern English-speakers), others in a range of ancient languages. Some are complete by modern standards (containing all 27 books), others are not. Some indeed, are church lectionaries which contain selected New Testament passages, arranged for reading in church through-out the liturgical year.

Even as a physical object, therefore, the New Testament of sixth-century Christians living in Constantinople, or of twelfth-century Christians in Armenia, would have looked and felt very different from an off-the-shelf English-language New Revised Standard Version (NRSV) or Jerusalem Bible (JB), and may have been put to very different uses. You can hold a modern printed New Testament in your hand, make marginal notes on its pages, and turn from one part to another relatively quickly. You can even buy a copy without breaking the bank, take it home, and read it quietly to yourself in the privacy of your study or the comfort of your armchair.

As a visit to the British Library will reveal, however, mass-produced, cheaply printed New Testaments are a fairly recent innovation. Prior to the fifteenth century, manuscripts of the New Testament had to be copied by hand (indeed, the word *manuscript* literally means something written by hand). This was an expensive, time-consuming task, and combined with general Christian illiteracy, meant that few individuals would have owned their own copy. New Testaments, on the whole, were the possession of monasteries, parish churches, and the wealthy and literate elite. Even when printing emerged on the scene, New Testaments would have remained relatively expensive, such that few (were they able to read) would have been in a position to purchase a copy. The New Testament, like the rest of the Bible, was a community possession. Some English churches still possess their own centuries-old communal Bible, chained to a lectern or desk to prevent theft.

When one moves back into the earlier centuries of the Church's life, things are even more complicated. In contrast to Judaism, which used parchment or papyrus scrolls for its sacred writings, the early Church soon opted for the codex (or leaf-book, the forerunner to our modern book). Positively, this meant that several writings could be copied and preserved together, whereas a long work might have to be spread across two or more scrolls. However, even codices were often limited in length. They might contain just the four gospels, or a collection of Paul's letters, or another combination; they would not necessarily contain all 27 writings. Indeed, in some cases they would contain writings not now included in our New Testament, or writings in a different order to the standard order (such issues to do with the New Testament canon are discussed at greater length in the companion volume to this one, *SCM Studyguide to the Books of the New Testament,* Chapter 13).

Another striking difference between our New Testaments and several of those New Testament manuscripts housed in the British Library is that the latter are written in languages other than English (for example, Greek, Latin, Syriac, Armenian). The legendary Anglican parishioner who famously quipped that 'If the Authorized Version was good enough for St Paul, it's good enough for me', would likely be traumatized by such a discovery! The original authors all wrote in the *koine* (or 'Common') Greek widely spoken throughout the Roman world. All other language versions, therefore, are translations, which means interpretations of the original. Some, indeed, are translations of translations. Moreover, while originally written in or translated into the vernacular (indeed, St Jerome's famous Bible translation, the Vulgate, is so called because it is a translation into the Latin 'vulgar tongue' of ordinary Western Christians), the New Testament has not always been preserved in the language of the people. One of the Reformers' protests against the hegemony of the Roman Catholic Church was that it persisted in reading and interpreting the New Testament scriptures in Latin, a foreign tongue to most Christians by the sixteenth century. Even today, some Eastern Christians hear the New Testament in older forms of their language (for example, Byzantine Greek, Church Slavonic).

Changes in Transmission

There are other reasons, too, why the New Testament has looked different at different times and in different places. First, the process of copying handwritten manuscripts has left its mark on our texts. If you have an annotated English New Testament, you will find in the margins or at the bottom of its pages a series of notes. Some of these are explanatory (aimed at helping the reader understand better), or pointing to parallels in the Old Testament or other New Testament books. But some of them reveal that the text of the New Testament itself has changed. These footnotes may be prefaced by 'Other ancient authorities read . . .' or some similar phrase.

In other words, over time errors have crept in or subtle changes have been made to the text, such that one of the tasks of the modern interpreter is to try to discern what the original reading would have been (these issues are explored in more detail in Chapter 4). Sometimes the variations are probably due to scribal error, perhaps the scribe's eye jumping from one line to another, or to a similar-sounding word. In other cases, the copyist may have deliberately corrected what he thought to be an inaccuracy in the manuscript before him. This may account, for example, for the variant reading 'in the prophets' rather than 'in the prophet Isaiah' at Mark 1.2, for the following verses quote not simply from Isaiah but also from Malachi (and the book of Exodus).

Second, explanatory marginal notes or footnotes have also affected the way in which people have understood the New Testament, and the Bible more generally. Though clearly secondary to the scriptural text, they can take on an authority on a par with that text, either because they derive from Church authorities or because they carry the 'authoritative voice' of the professional biblical scholar. The *Scofield Study Bible,* an edition of the Authorized Version with explanatory notes by C. I. Scofield, has become the definitive version of huge numbers of American Protestant Christians, who read and interpret the Bible through the lens provided by Scofield himself. In the pre-printing period, indeed, marginal comments may have found their way into the New Testament text itself by a scribe not clearly distinguishing between the two. Some scholars think that the phrase at the end of John 4.9 ('Jews do not share things in common with Samaritans') is a case in point, for it is lacking in some manuscripts.

Third, how one divides up the text makes one view the text differently. The earliest manuscripts of the New Testament books did not even have gaps between the words, let alone paragraph breaks and punctuation such as full stops and question marks. Our modern New Testaments, however, have chapter and verse divisions, as well as punctuation and paragraphs (the result of decisions made by editors and interpreters). The chapter divisions generally followed today are attributable to a thirteenth-century Archbishop of Canterbury, Stephen Langton (d. 1228), who is believed to have devised the system while lecturing at the University of Paris. The system of verse divisions is even later, first appearing in the 1551 Greek and Latin New Testament of Robert Estienne (or Stephanus). Alternative systems of chapter divisions circulated in the earlier period.

But chapter and verse divisions are not always obvious, and might even on occasion obscure the most obvious sense. Commentators on Matthew's Gospel, for example, regularly think that a new crucial stage of the narrative begins at 4.12, with Jesus entering into Galilee. This is somewhat obscured by the chapter divisions at 4.1 and 5.1. Similarly, a new section of the book of Revelation may begin not at 12.1, with the appearance of the woman clothed with the sun, but one verse earlier at 11.19. Moreover, not all modern translations agree as to where paragraph breaks ought to fall, or whether there should be gaps on the printed page to illustrate textual issues (for example after Mark 16.8, highlighting the discrepancies between the various ancient manuscripts as to how Mark's Gospel ends).

To do

Look at your own copy of the New Testament (or the various copies you possess). Is it bound on its own, or together with the 'Old Testament'? What difference does this make? Is it 'annotated', that is, with explanatory footnotes? If so, how far do these determine how you read? Are the words of Jesus printed in red (a 'red-letter' Bible)? What might this suggest? What titles does your version give to the individual books? Do these differ from other versions of the New Testament?

Reception of the New Testament

A final way in which the New Testament has often been experienced differently is linked not so much to the written or printed text but to the variety of ways in which it has been communicated. For much of Christian history, the New Testament is something that has been heard, or visualized, rather than read. Partly, this reflects the widespread illiteracy of ordinary Christians; partly, it reflects the use to which the New Testament has been put in the Church.

First, many Christians have primarily heard the New Testament read out loud. Indeed, this seems to be the procedure envisaged by New Testament writers, who speak of 'the reader' in the singular as the one who would read the text to the assembled congregation (for example, Mark 13.14; Revelation 1.3). Hearing a book in a group has a very different effect from a silent, individual reading. Second, parts of the New Testament, especially the gospels, have been acted out during a religious service or as an extra-liturgical drama. Among the most famous survivors are the Oberammergau Passion Play and the various mystery plays that have been revived in English cathedral cities. Many churches will re-enact Christ's entry into Jerusalem on Palm Sunday, or stage a dramatic reading of John's passion account on Good Friday. These re-enactments highlight the dramatic effect of the biblical story, which may be obscured by a private reading of the New Testament, and the invitation to the congregation or audience to enter into the story and make it their own.

Alternatively, the New Testament has been a visual experience. The narrative sections (notably the gospels, Acts and Revelation) have made an impact in icons, frescoes, altarpieces and devotional paintings. Indeed, our art galleries are jam packed with art works originally designed for churches, and so somewhat 'out of context'. Though not always treated as such, unnamed icon painters, or the architects of our medieval cathedrals (influenced by the description of the heavenly Jerusalem in Revelation 21—22), or artists such as Rembrandt and Caravaggio, have been among the greatest and most influential interpreters of the New Testament. Recent developments in biblical scholarship have brought their contribution back onto the scholarly agenda. Further discussion of the visual and dramatic interpretation of the New Testament can be found in Chapter 11 below.

Reflection

List the different ways in which you have been exposed to the New Testament (for example, private devotional reading; private study; hearing a public reading; watching a film or play based on a New Testament book; looking at a painting of a New Testament scene), and the places where these have happened. What different effects have these different types of exposure had on you?

What is in a Name?

There is one obvious question (perhaps too obvious!) that we have not yet attempted to answer: why is this diverse collection of writings called the *New Testament*? Names are illuminating, whether they be names given to children or to books. So what lies behind this particular name? This question can be approached from at least three perspectives.

First, where does the phrase itself come from? The earliest recorded example is actually found in the Old Testament, in a passage from the prophet Jeremiah, dating from the sixth century BCE (= Before the Common Era, an alternative way of expressing the more familiar BC):

> 'The days are surely coming,' says the Lord, 'when I will make a new covenant with the house of Israel and the house of Judah.' (Jeremiah 31.31)

The phrase translated here by the New Revised Standard Version (NRSV) as 'new covenant' could also mean 'new testament' (*diathēkē kainē* in the Greek Septuagint (LXX)). Clearly the prophet Jeremiah is not thinking about our 27 books, which will not emerge for another 600 years! Instead, he looks to a time when the covenant or special relationship between God and his people Israel will be renewed, overlooking the people's previous infidelity.

Nevertheless, Jeremiah's phrase is taken up, and applied to Jesus, in the New Testament itself. In two accounts of his last supper, for example (the longer form of Luke 22.20 and 1 Corinthians 11.25), Jesus is recorded as talking about a 'new covenant' in his blood, that is a new relationship established by his death. Paul elsewhere contrasts the 'old covenant' associated with the Jewish synagogue with the 'new covenant' of Christians (2 Corinthians 3.6, 14). The letter to the Hebrews quotes the Jeremiah passage, interpreting it to mean the replacement of the older covenant by the new covenant established by Christ (Hebrews 8.6–13). Apparently, Christ's life and death have established a new covenant, a new relationship, between God and his people (a people now made up not only of Jews but also of non-Jews).

The second question, then, is why this term 'covenant' or 'testament' came to be applied to this disparate collection of writings. In what sense are these books a 'testament', 'covenant' or 'pact' (Greek *diathēkē*; Latin *testamentum*)? Perhaps our current English usage may help. We still speak of a 'last will and testament' to describe a person's last wishes. The Greek word *diathēkē* means both 'covenant' and 'will'. In simplest terms, the 'New Testament' is the written testimony both to the new relationship established between God and humanity in Jesus Christ, and to the will of the dying Jesus for a community which would express that new relationship in concrete terms.

Third, in what way is it 'new'? This question has been thrown into sharper relief by recent scholarship's acute awareness of the anti-Semitic potential of the New Testament writings, which emerged historically out of a period of intense debate and mutual distrust between early Christians and the Jewish synagogue. To call these writings 'the New Testament' obviously juxtaposes them to an 'Old Testament' (the Christian description of those scriptures shared in common by Christians and Jews, though Hebrew and Greek canons differ). Some scholars have urged us to find alternative titles: John Goldingay suggests 'First Testament' and 'Second Testament'.[1] But what precisely is implied in the juxtaposition of 'old' and 'new'? That the new is better than the old? That the new has superseded the old? That the old is to be preferred to the new-fangled latecomer? That both old and new are needed for a complete understanding of this relationship between God and God's people?

This debate, it must be admitted, is as old as Christianity itself. A story about Jesus preserved in the first three gospels serves to illustrate the point. It is essentially a 'conflict story' in which Jesus debates with his religious opponents over the practice of fasting (Matthew 9.14–17 // Mark 2.18–22 // Luke 5.33–9). But the really interesting point is how Mark (probably the earliest account), Matthew and Luke conclude this story differently:

Matthew 9.17	*Mark 2.22*	*Luke 5.37–39*
Neither is new wine put into old wineskins; otherwise, the skins burst, and the wine is spilled, and the skins are destroyed;	And no one puts new wine into old wineskins; otherwise, the wine will burst the skins, and the wine is lost, and so are the skins;	And no one puts new wine into old wineskins; otherwise, the new wine will burst the skins and will be spilled, and the skins will be destroyed.
but new wine is put into fresh wineskins, *and so both are preserved.*	but one puts new wine into fresh wineskins.	But new wine must be put into fresh wineskins. *And no one after drinking old wine desires new wine, but says, 'The old is good.'*

Mark's ending seems to stress the radical disjunction between old and new: what has happened in Christ is so radically new that the old cannot contain it ('but one puts new wine into fresh wineskins', Mark 2.22). The Jewish Matthew, on the other hand, wants to stress the essential continuity between the old and the new. The coming of Christ fulfils, but does not supersede, that which came before. Hence he adds to Mark's ending the words: 'and so both are preserved' (Matthew 9.17). Finally, Luke rather puzzlingly concludes with words that seem to point to the superiority of the old over the new (Luke 5.39). It is perhaps a recognition that, rightly or wrongly, some people view 'new' things as actually inferior to the 'old', the tried and tested.

This tension, then, is inherent within Christianity. However, there is one further factor that needs to be borne in mind: the Christian Bible contains *both* Old *and* New Testaments. Though one second-century theologian, Marcion, suggested that Christians should ditch the Jewish scriptures, the Church has rejected that option. Whatever the nuances of the adjective 'new', the Christian usage of 'New Testament' cannot mean that the 'Old Testament' is to be regarded as superfluous.

Reflection

Think of the different ways in which we talk about something being 'new'. In what ways might the New Testament be 'new'?

Why do People Read it?

Just as over the centuries different people, and groups of people, have understood the New Testament to mean slightly different things, and have read or heard it in different ways, so too their reasons for reading have differed. Believers have read it because they want to learn about Jesus, or because they regard it as the word of life. Some have approached it rather like a textbook, perhaps a compendium of Church teaching (authoritatively interpreted by the Church leaders). Others have scoured its pages (particularly its last section!) for information about human history, or about the end of the world.

Still others have read it for the beauty of its prose or poetry (particularly in more 'literary' translations), or to be inspired in their artistic endeavours. In our post-Christian world, people's reasons for reading the New Testament are even more diverse. Here are some possibilities:

- They are reading these books as holy scripture, bringing them closer to Christ.
- Their faith has been shaken by a traumatic personal event, and they are seeking an answer to their questions.
- They are in search of meaning for their life, and are exploring a range of religious and philosophical traditions.
- They are critics of Christianity in particular and religion in general, who want their objections to be better informed.
- They want to learn about the history of earliest Christianity.
- They have an exam to pass at the end of the year.
- They are aware of the cultural importance of the New Testament (such that, for example, one cannot understand many of the paintings in the National Gallery without some background knowledge).
- They want to appreciate these writings as classic literature.
- They are fascinated with the historical person Jesus of Nazareth, or with a figure of the early Church, such as St Paul.

Moreover, the same readers can read and study it in different contexts. You might be an atheist who is nevertheless an historian of early Christianity. You could appreciate the literary merits of the New Testament while also wanting to understand better Caravaggio's *Supper at Emmaus* (interpreting a scene from Luke 24) or John Martin's *The Great Day of His Wrath* (based on the book of Revelation, and housed in London's Tate Britain). You could be both a believer and a professional biblical scholar. Indeed, for centuries some of the greatest biblical exegetes were also pastors and preachers (for example, Augustine of Hippo, John Chrysostom, Thomas Aquinas). This may seem strange, given the increasing focus of biblical studies in non-denominational universities and theology faculties. Some Christians speak as if 'professional' New Testament scholars are actively hostile to Christianity, or at best raising questions that undermine the authority of the New Testament. But Christian history shows that far from being incompatible, the two go well hand in hand.

Of course, the richness of the New Testament and the variety of reasons why people read and study it means that Christians and Jews, atheists and agnostics, literary critics and historians, lay people and professionals, all have a part to play. The New Testament writings cannot be the sole preserve of the churches. Nevertheless, one growing criticism of New Testament scholarship, coming from professional scholars who are also Christians, is that it has lost touch with the life of the Church. Whereas in the past critical scholarship often challenged the claims of Church hierarchies to possess the definitive interpretation, the academy (scholars working in the university) is now accused of making the same claims for itself. A number of disparate voices – from those who are both academic New Testament scholars and practising Christians of different traditions – are calling for the gulf between Church and academy to be bridged once again, partly by relearning older methods of exegesis.[2] One of these voices, the American Catholic Luke Timothy Johnson, reminds us of the medieval adage that the quest for knowledge (*scientia*) should go hand in hand with the quest for wisdom (*sapientia*).

Such critics are not calling for a straightforward return to pre-critical ways of reading. Nor are they disputing the right of non-Christian, agnostic or atheist scholars to interpret the New Testament, still less denying the insights that many of these have given. However, they do want to make space within the academy for a New Testament scholarship that is both scholarly and ecclesial (that is, attending to the life and faith of the Church). The question of the relationship between scholarship and faith commitment will be explored further in the next chapter.

Reflection

What reasons do you have for studying the New Testament? Can you add any to the list above? Don't be surprised if you list more than one reason.

A Diverse Collection

Let us think a bit more about the contents of the New Testament. As noted briefly above, it is actually a compilation of very diverse writings, dated (broadly) to the second half of the first century CE. This is a rough rule of thumb: precise dating of the individual writings is very difficult, with often wide discrepancies between scholars (the earliest books have been dated as early as the 30s/40s, and the latest sometimes pushed well into the second century). They can be classified as follows:

- Four accounts of Jesus' life, death and resurrection (*the gospels*). One of these (*John*) diverges considerably in content from the other three (*Matthew, Mark* and *Luke*). However, a careful reader will notice marked differences in details (and sometimes in content) between these three also. Some of these differences, and the reasons why all four are preserved in the New Testament, will be explored in Chapter 5.
- A book of *Acts*, supposedly (by its later title) '*of the Apostles*', which is actually focused first on Peter and then on Paul (who to some in the New Testament was not an apostle). On the surface at least, Acts looks like a history of the early Church, though it may be a more complicated text. It begins by referring to the author's 'first book', addressed like this one to someone called 'Theophilus'. This 'first book' must be the Gospel according to Luke, although the two volumes are separated in our New Testament by John's Gospel. Thus in modern scholarship, Luke and Acts are regularly interpreted together.
- A series of letters, some to communities, some to individuals, some circular (to be circulated to a wide geographical area), some specific (responding to problems in precise locations). The majority claim to be written by *Paul*, although others either claim to be, or were later attributed to, Jesus' original followers (*Peter, John*) or members of his family (*James, Jude*). The letters attributed to Paul (some of which may not be by Paul himself) are generally called the *Pauline corpus*. The seven attributed to James, Peter, John and Jude are known as the *Catholic* (or 'general') *Epistles*, since they are not on the whole addressed to specific named individuals or communities.

Although modern readers are familiar with the letter form, and therefore one might expect the New Testament letters to be easiest to interpret, we are faced with one obvious problem. They only allow us access to one side of an ancient conversation (we do not hear the other side, and attempts to 'fill in the gaps' are inevitably fragmentary). Moreover, we should not underestimate the cultural and linguistic gulf between them and us. These writings emerge from a very different age and society, and were originally written not in English but in an ancient form of Greek.

- Possibly a homily or two: *Hebrews* and perhaps *1 John*. Though both of these are regularly called 'letters', they lack the conventions of an ancient letter (either at the beginning, in the case of Hebrews, or both at the beginning and the end, in the case of 1 John). They may be nearer in form to a homily or sermon, or (in the case of 1 John) a theological treatise.
- An 'apocalypse' (*Revelation*), from the Greek word meaning 'revelation' or 'unveiling'. Apocalypses are Jewish and early Christian narrative works that purport to unveil heavenly secrets through dreams, heavenly journeys or angelic visitation. The mysteries are often clothed in symbolic visions featuring angels, demons and fantastic creatures, and numbers are given symbolic significance. Though probably familiar to early Christians, a book like Revelation is particularly difficult for the modern mind-set.

These very different types of books will require different interpretative approaches, and it is important for students of the New Testament to be aware of their literary 'genre'. Even today, we appreciate almost instinctively that a poem should not be interpreted in the same way as the weather forecast, and that the 'Dear Mr X' in a letter from the bank manager does not convey the same meaning as the 'Dear Y' in a letter to a loved one. So too we need particular rules for understanding different types of ancient writings.

However, differences in literary form are not confined to the macro-level. Even within individual books, on a micro-scale, a number of different literary types can be found. The Gospel according to Mark, for example, contains within it stories of Jesus healing and stories of Jesus debating with his opponents. It contains both narrative and teaching. It contains narratives which claim to describe events in Jesus' ministry (for example, Jesus being baptized by John the Baptist) and fictional narratives (the stories that Jesus told, like the parable of the sower). It includes a short, matter-of-fact account of the call of Jesus' first four disciples, and a long, detailed account of Jesus' last days and hours, interpreted in the light of the Jewish scriptures. Nor is this combination of literary types confined to the narrative parts of the New Testament. Occasionally in his letters, Paul seems to include a quotation from an early Christian hymn or creed, and these need to be handled rather differently than comments about his travel plans. Part of what is involved in studying the New Testament is to discern which skills are appropriate to its different parts.

To do

Look through a daily newspaper. Try to identify different literary 'genres' (for example, letters; editorial; weather forecast; obituaries; advertisements). Write down what distinguishes each. What are the different ways in which you interpret these different genres?

Why is it in the order it is?

If the genre of the individual writings affects interpretation, so too (though often unconsciously) does the order in which they are preserved. Why is the New Testament in the order in which it is? The first thing to note here is that the standard order has not always been so firmly fixed. Indeed, in times when different parts of the New Testament were bound separately in different codices, that is not particularly surprising. Some ancient codices of the New Testament (for example, the Codex Sinaiticus, dated to the fourth century and now housed in the British Library) preserve a rather different order, as does the canonical list given by St Athanasius in his Festal Letter of 367 CE (the earliest list to include all 27 of our writings). Sinaiticus also includes two non-canonical writings:

Standard Order	*Codex Sinaiticus (4th cent)*	*Athanasius (367)*
Matthew	Matthew	Matthew
Mark	Mark	Mark
Luke	Luke	Luke
John	John	John
Acts	Romans	Acts
Romans	1 Corinthians	*James*
1 Corinthians	2 Corinthians	*1 Peter*
2 Corinthians	Galatians	*2 Peter*
Galatians	Ephesians	*1 John*
Ephesians	Philippians	*2 John*
Philippians	Colossians	*3 John*
Colossians	1 Thessalonians	*Jude*
1 Thessalonians	2 Thessalonians	Romans
2 Thessalonians	*Hebrews*	1 Corinthians
1 Timothy	1 Timothy	2 Corinthians
2 Timothy	2 Timothy	Galatians
Titus	Titus	Ephesians
Philemon	Philemon	Philippians
Hebrews	*Acts*	Colossians
James	James	1 Thessalonians
1 Peter	1 Peter	2 Thessalonians
2 Peter	2 Peter	*Hebrews*
1 John	1 John	1 Timothy
2 John	2 John	2 Timothy
3 John	3 John	Titus
Jude	Jude	Philemon
Revelation	Revelation	Revelation
	Epistle of Barnabas	
	Shepherd of Hermas	

Nevertheless, there is some logic to what became the established order:

- It is largely chronological in terms of subjects (Jesus, then the story of the early Church, then Paul followed by other writers, climaxing in the End).
- The length of the books also comes into play. In the Pauline corpus, the order of the letters to the churches moves from the longest to the shortest (Romans – 2 Thessalonians), though allowing for letters to the same churches to be grouped together (1 and 2 Corinthians; 1 and 2 Thessalonians). The same principle seems to govern the order of the letters to individuals (1 and 2 Timothy; Titus; Philemon), and may also be reflected in the Catholic Epistles.
- When books are found in a different order, they are generally still 'grouped' together (for example, the 'Catholic Epistles' precede the 'Pauline Corpus' in Athanasius' list); Acts – a 'stand-alone' text once separated from Luke's Gospel – shifts its position in the Codex Sinaiticus.
- The one exception is Hebrews, which in both Sinaiticus and Athanasius is found between 2 Thessalonians and 1 Timothy, that is, firmly within the Pauline corpus, reflecting its early attribution to Paul in the Eastern Church. This is reflected in its title in the Authorized Version: 'the Epistle of Paul the Apostle to the Hebrews'.
- The distinctive groupings may reflect the historical process by which the 27 writings came to be collected: for example, a collection of Paul's letters; a separate collection of the four gospels, or the gospels and Acts.
- The grouping of all four gospels together reflects an early victory within the Church: the New Testament canon requires all four, together but not merged into each other. However, while the order Matthew, Mark, Luke and John is almost universally found, there are exceptions: the fifth-century Codex Bezae (a bilingual version in Latin and Greek) has the unusual order Matthew, John, Luke and Mark.

What we can be fairly sure of, however, is that although the standard order has these writings in approximatly chronological order of *subject matter*, they are not ordered chronologically in terms of *writing*. Paul's letters were almost certainly written prior to the gospels, while Revelation may actually be earlier than John or Acts.

To do

Compare the three canonical lists given above. What books are listed in a different order? What might that suggest about the way they were viewed by those who arranged them in this order? Their importance, authorship and dating?

How to Proceed

The preceding discussion should leave you in no doubt as to one thing: the New Testament is a complex phenomenon. It has looked different, meant different things to different people, and even today can be approached from many different angles and studied for many different reasons. Therefore, studying the New Testament is going to be a complex, multifaceted task. But though challenging, I hope you will see it as a challenge full of exciting possibilities. In the remaining chapters, we shall attempt to sketch out some of the ways in which these books have been studied, and provide tools for interpreting the books ourselves. It will require at different times the skills of the historian and the literary critic, the philosopher and the linguist, the artist and the archaeologist, the geographer and the palaeographer, the theologian and the mystic. It is a task, moreover, on which the sceptic, the searcher and the believer may embark together, and be prepared to learn from one another. I hope you will see that it is a journey worth embarking upon.

2

Where is Meaning to be Found?

The Elusiveness of Meaning

Before we begin to look in more detail at ways of reading the New Testament, it is worth reflecting on the question of meaning. When we read, or speak, or listen, we are in the business of communication. We want to convey meaning by what we write or say, or to elicit meaning from what we read or hear. Basically, we want to understand, and we want to be understood. Sometimes, it is painfully obvious that we have failed to grasp the meaning adequately. We may be reading a particularly difficult book, or just a badly written book, and be left scratching our heads in bewilderment. We may be talking with someone whose first language is not English, and who is struggling to articulate what they mean.

But even when we are talking with a native English speaker, or reading what they have written, grasping the meaning of their words requires some effort. Words themselves can mean several different things. Take, for example, the English word 'fine': it can be a description of the weather, or of someone's state of health, or of thin hair; but it can also refer to a sum of money payable for a parking offence. In spoken English, the fact that different words are pronounced the same can cause further ambiguity: for example, 'bough' and 'bow', or 'sight' and 'site'. In written English, 'Polish' (pertaining to Poland) and 'polish' (of the Mr Sheen variety) look the same, though are pronounced differently.

So in some cases, hearing a word will help make better sense of it; in other cases, seeing it written will clarify which word is being used. But in all cases, we need to know its *context*. Words find their meaning in the context in which they appear. The more we know about the context, the more intelligible a word or phrase will be. This will still not rule out misunderstanding or ambiguity: cultural factors, or deliberate double entendres, need to be taken into account. But we are on the way to grasping its meaning.

We are 'on the way', but we still have a long way to go. Reading or hearing words in a sequence may convey a certain meaning. But the wider context of that sequence (the dialogue, or the chapter, of which they are part) is crucial for confirming whether or not our initial hunch is correct. The meaning of 'Jim is in a tight corner' will differ according to whether the wider scenario is of a small and crowded room, or of a man who has got himself into trouble. If the words are spoken, the tone of voice will convey whether the speaker is serious, or being sarcastic or ironic, or asking a question rather than making a statement. When we are dealing with written texts, we cannot hear the tone of voice of the author, and so a certain ambiguity remains.

A New Testament Example

Let us take an example from the New Testament itself:

> We played the flute for you, and you did not dance;
> we wailed, and you did not weep.

The context in which certain words are used in this sentence, and the way they are juxtaposed with other words, helps us rule out some possible meanings. For example, after the verb 'we played', the word 'flute' is likely to refer not to a champagne glass but to a musical instrument! Given its place in the sentence, 'dance' here is a verb rather than a noun. Moreover, the sentence itself is grammatical and therefore intelligible English (unlike a sentence such as 'cat in were ship encyclopaedia eats how', which we would describe as 'meaningless').

It is possible, therefore, to come to an initial understanding of what this sentence means. It has something to do with people (the 'we') playing in-struments and wailing, and suggests that the response of the 'you' is unex-pected or even disappointing. Of course, we are at a disadvantage here: we can't hear the tone of voice of the speaker, so we don't know for sure whether these words are spoken in anger, or sympathy, or with humour.

Moreover, there is a wider context which we do not yet have: its literary context within the New Testament. Once we learn that this passage is Luke 7.32, we can look at this wider literary context:

> To what then will I compare the people of this generation, and what are they like? They are like children sitting in the market-place and calling to one another,
>> 'We played the flute for you, and you did not dance;
>> we wailed, and you did not weep.'
> For John the Baptist has come eating no bread and drinking no wine, and you say, 'He has a demon'; the Son of Man has come eating and drinking, and you say, 'Look, a glutton and a drunkard, a friend of tax-collectors and sinners!' Nevertheless, wisdom is vindicated by all her children. (Luke 7.31–5)

Knowing this context forces us to reassess our initial understanding. In Luke 7, Jesus is talking about himself and John the Baptist, and the con-trasting reactions of the people to these two figures. John, the locust and honey eating ascetic, is accused of having a demon; Jesus, the party animal, of being a glutton and a drunk. It is a no-win situation: the people are fickle. In this context, our sample passage is not a literal statement, but a simile. The people of Jesus' and John's day are not literal flute-players or wailers at all. But they are *like* fickle children, who play at weddings and funerals in the marketplace, and complain when others don't play along with them, or don't keep up with the change of game. The *sense* of the juxtaposition of the words ('you' are not responding expectedly or appropriately to our flute playing and wailing) now finds a more specific *meaning* in the wider context of the passage (in their reaction to John and Jesus, the people are like children who are never satisfied with how others (adults?) respond to their games).

Yet is that all that can be said about the meaning of the passage? Many New Testament scholars would indeed want to see this as the meaning: that is, what the first-century author (known in tradition as Luke) intended to convey by telling the story in this way. This takes seriously the gulf between us and the author and original readers (or hearers) of the gospel. It recognizes that some knowledge of their cultural setting is necessary if we are not to interpret inappropriately: that, for example, flutes were played at weddings and dirge-singers engaged for funerals. It acknowledges the anachronism of the alternative interpretation of 'flutes': calling champagne glasses 'flutes' is a decidedly modern phenomenon. Alternatively, the meaning may be what the text itself conveys (recognizing the uncertainty of knowing precisely what an ancient author might have intended).

But is that enough? Can this passage mean more? When people talk about finding meaning for their lives, they intend more than interpreting a sentence intelligibly. Many readers of the New Testament are interested not simply in what the passage or book in question meant to the person who wrote it, but also what it might mean *for them* and their lives. Mark Allan Powell makes the helpful distinction between meaning as *message* and meaning as *effect*.[3] New Testament scholars often understand meaning primarily in terms of the message conveyed, the point being made in a particular passage. But, argues Powell, there is a more *emotive* or *affective* aspect to meaning which many are looking for in the New Testament. It is akin to asking of a film or an abstract painting: 'What do you make of this?' or 'What does this mean?' To come back to our example, the meaning of the flute-player and wailing passage might also have to do with the *impact* it has on the readers or hearers. It might lead people to ask where they stand in relation to Jesus and John, whether they are like fickle children (and so to be allied with 'the people of this generation'), and so to change their commitments and their lives.

Reflection

Think of two or three different scenarios in which you might ask about the meaning of something (for example, a mathematical problem; a painting; a novel; a tragic event; a plan of the London underground). What different kinds of meaning might be involved?

Three Approaches

Meaning, then, is rather elusive, not least because 'meaning' conveys different things to different people. In order to understand how New Testament scholarship grapples with this issue, it may be helpful to think in terms of three basic approaches. These are:

- *author*-centred,
- *text*-centred,
- *reader*-centred.

As we shall see, these are not necessarily watertight. Those who focus mainly on the text, for example, do not necessarily ignore the historical context in which that text was written. Other interpreters will pay attention both to the shape of a text and to the dynamic interplay between that text and the contemporary reader. But the three terms denote the primary focus of different ways of reading and seeking meaning.

Author-centred approaches, which use historical-critical methods, regard the intention of the original author of a book as determinative. The meaning of the passage above is essentially what Luke the evangelist intended to convey. In other words, to understand a New Testament passage, you need to attend as much as possible to the context of the original author, how he or she has used and reshaped the sources and traditions available, and what he or she seems to be saying to the original recipients or hearers of the text (this kind of approach will be explored in more detail in Chapter 6).

This is sometimes called a *diachronic* approach (from the Greek 'through time'): that is, one that uses the text to uncover the earlier time of the author, or explore the various sources used by that author. Another way of conceptualizing it is an approach which uses the text as *a window*. Looking through the window, one can glimpse something of the early Christians, their life, their concerns, and especially the life and concerns of the individual New Testament writers.

Others prefer a text-centred approach. That is, they study the shape of a book as a whole, watch for clues within the text as to how it should be divided, or how readers might be expected to respond. If it is a narrative, they may focus on aspects such as plot development, characterization, and point of view. Narrative criticism is particularly interested in these kinds of questions.[4] Meaning, in other words, is embedded in the text itself. If author-centred readings are 'diachronic', text-centred approaches are *synchronic* (from the Greek 'with time' or 'the same time'). The text is now treated not as a window onto an earlier period, but as *a story-world* to be entered into, or a *tapestry* to be examined in its entirety.

A third type of approach focuses on the reader. It recognizes that no two readers are exactly alike, and will therefore respond in somewhat different ways. Indeed, the same reader will not read the same text in exactly the same way twice, just as every performance of a symphony by Mozart or Beethoven

---

Table 2: Looking again at Luke 7.31–5.

Author-centred readings will ask questions like:
- Why did Luke present the contemporaries of Jesus and John in this way?
- What is he wanting to say to his intended audience?
- Has he altered the ending as found in Matthew ('wisdom is vindicated by her deeds', Matthew 11.19) to 'by all her children', and if so, why?

Text-centred readings will ask questions like:
- How does this passage fit into its surrounding literary context?
- What has the text told us before about 'the people of this generation'? About John the Baptist and 'the Son of Man'?
- Which characters appear in a positive light, and which in a negative?

Reader-centred readings will ask questions like:
- Why do I identify with particular characters in the story?
- Might this passage read differently if approached from the perspective of the children?
- Doesn't this passage subvert Paul's claim (1 Corinthians 6.10) that drunkards will not inherit the kingdom of God?

is a unique experience. For such interpreters, the text itself does not 'mean' anything until it is read by a human reader. Without the human act of reading, it remains a dead letter, an inanimate object. Meaning, then, is to be found in the dynamic between the text and the reader, such that there cannot be only one, definitive meaning. Because every reader is unique, and every act of reading unique, a text is open to a multiplicity of readings. In this kind of approach, the text is *a mirror*, in which something of our own reflection is to be found. We always bring something of ourselves to the act of interpretation. Text- and reader-centred approaches will be looked at again in Chapters 7 and 9.

To do

Read Matthew 15.21–8 (the story of the Canaanite woman). Write down two or three questions that you think an author-centred approach would want to ask. Do the same again for text- and reader-centred approaches (you might also want to look at the parallel version at Mark 7.24–30).

Reading in a Community

These three models are helpful for understanding how different people seek meaning in the New Testament texts (even if they sometimes overlap). However, they could be criticized for being too individualistic. Yet the reality is that none of us reads, or hears, or indeed performs any other activity alone, or in a vacuum. In particular, when we read the New Testament writings, we do so as members of a community (or for most of us, as members of several overlapping communities). Some of us approach the New Testament as members of particular Christian traditions, which have historically read New Testament passages in particular ways. The Roman Catholic tradition, for example, reads Jesus' words to Peter at Matthew 16.18 ('you are Peter, and on this rock I will build my church') as bearing fruit in the institution of the papacy. The Lutheran tradition would regard Paul's teaching about 'justification by faith' as the key to the New Testament revelation. Some read primarily as professional biblical scholars, often further subdivided according to what kind of approach they take to the text (for example, historical critics; narrative critics). Some of us belong to both communities (Church and academy), and attempt to hold the two together. Moreover, all of us are members of the human community, and many human cultures have been profoundly shaped, often in unconscious ways, by the New Testament. Even if we are atheistic critics, our atheism gives us a particular stance vis-à-vis these writings. Moreover, we may also be influenced by the New Testament's impact upon our wider culture. Whoever we are, we read and interpret as communities.

This much is unavoidable. Nor is it necessarily a bad thing. Indeed, there are advantages in searching for meaning as part of a community. One's particular readings can be challenged by others in that reading community, and one can benefit from the wisdom of that community's reading of the New Testament in the past (for a Christian community, that may be centuries of accumulated wisdom). Of course, every community is limited in its capacity to understand, and may be blind to particular readings. It is vital to ensure, therefore, that different reading communities dialogue with one another, and are prepared to learn from one another, rather than engaging in private and evermore esoteric internal conversations. The ecumenical movement among Christians, or the greater collaboration between Jewish and Christian scholars, are examples of where such conversations have begun.

Recently, the American Episcopalian scholar William Countryman has proposed a model for understanding how we read and interpret biblical texts that takes this community aspect more seriously. He suggests a triangular model in which the three apexes are the text, the interpreter and the community of readers, without whom the act of interpretation will be a fleeting and isolated activity. Eschewing the tendency towards fragmentation in New Testament scholarship (in which author-, text- and reader-centred approaches are often opposed to one another), he calls for a more dynamic conversation between the three points of the triangle.[5]

The Role of the Author

Let us return for the moment to author-centred readings. Those who advocate such readings remind us that, whatever subsequent readings of texts emerge in later generations, there was an original meaning that the original author was wanting to convey to those for whom he or she was writing. The author of Matthew's Gospel was certainly not thinking of Pope Benedict XVI when he had Jesus call Peter a 'rock'. Nor was John of Patmos foretelling the formation of the European Union, or of the World Council of Churches, when he described the seven-headed, ten-horned beast in Revelation 13. His claim to be recounting 'what must soon take place' for the sake of seven first-century Christian communities (Revelation 1.1, 4) seems to rule this out. Attending to this 'primary' meaning, they claim, ought to be the point of departure for all other readings. For some, indeed, what the author intended is the only meaning of the passage. For others, it provides constraints on later rereadings which prevent people from 'making the text mean anything at all'.

This is a good starting point. After all, few would claim that the meaning of *Harry Potter and the Half-Blood Prince* has nothing to do with J. K. Rowling and her intention in writing. Nevertheless, there is one crucial difference between the Potter books and an ancient text such as the Gospel of Luke: we no longer have direct access to the author of the latter. Indeed, we do not know for sure the identity or social background of that author (the title 'according to Luke' may not have been attached to this book before the second century CE). We can question Joanne Rowling about her intentions; in fact, these have been preserved for posterity through published interviews. But we do not have direct access to the intentions of 'Luke' (apart from the general ones set out in his Prologue: Luke 1.1–4).

So while an attempt to 'get close to' an original author's intention may be a good thing, we need to be more modest in our aims. Given that we can no longer interrogate a John or a Paul, to clarify ambiguities or fill in gaps, we can never be sure we have got it right. Nor can we hear their tone of voice, or see their facial reactions. There will be things an ancient author could assume his or her audience would know – for example, the identity of 'the disciple whom Jesus loved', or what has happened in Galatia prior to Paul's writing – at which we can only guess (even if these are educated guesses, making good sense of the surviving evidence). If even modern authors can be misunderstood in what they write, how much more so a dead author of a very different time and culture.

There is one further reason why the quest for authorial intention should not be the only focus in the quest for meaning. That is, human authors may convey more than they consciously intend. By this I don't mean that they are misunderstood (though they frequently are!). Rather, I am thinking more positively of that experience of realizing that your words convey more than you were aware of in the act of writing. Novelists regularly speak of characters forming on the page, or of plots developing in unexpected directions. A poet's work may have a capacity to move and inspire far beyond the conscious thought processes of the poet. In the New Testament itself, the book of Revelation claims to be based on visions received by John on the island of Patmos. If we take this seriously, we have a book where authorial intention is much further in the background than, say, Luke's Gospel or Paul's letter to the Philippians. Rather, the author's influence may be more unconscious (even to himself!); he leaves his mark on what he writes, but not always in an explicit or conscious manner.

For Christians, such a recognition can go hand in hand with a doctrine of inspiration. In Christian tradition, these writings are not simply words of human authors, but the word of God. Traditionally, this has not meant (as in some contemporary versions of inspiration) that the particularity and cultural constraints of the human authors have been overridden or set aside. However, it has wanted to claim that in and through these human words, the Spirit has the capacity to breathe and to speak, in a way which can transcend that authorial particularity. Chapter 10 will discuss further this explicitly *theological* understanding of the New Testament (from the Greek for talk (*logos*) about God (*theos*)).

The Text and the Reader

Text-centred approaches acknowledge this capacity of texts to mean more than the conscious intention of their human authors. Connections between different parts of the text, or allusions to other texts (in the case of the New

Testament, most especially to Old Testament writings), which may have been unconscious to the author become explicit in the written text. Moreover, literary texts exhibit concrete features that suggest a particular way of reading, even when explicit reference to an author's intention is not evident. They contain markers that suggest how the text should be broken up, or which indicate the high points; they employ rhetoric, and rhetorical techniques such as irony; they exhibit a particular 'point of view' that suggests how readers ought to respond.

When the Pharisees (one of the religious groupings in Jewish Palestine during the life of Jesus) occur in Matthew's Gospel, for example, their generally negative presentation suggests that readers and audiences should view them in a negative light. They are opposed to Jesus, who is the 'hero' of the story; indeed, in Matthew 23 they are described (along with 'the scribes') as 'hypocrites' no less than six times. That does not, of course, prevent a reader (unexpectedly) from viewing them more sympathetically, particularly if she knows that historically the Pharisees were more diverse and better regarded than Matthew's portrayal implies. But it reflects the 'point of view' of the narrative.

Reader-oriented interpreters highlight the occurrences of such 'unexpected' readings as the sympathetic assessment of the Pharisees in Matthew. Readers, after all, being individuals, are notoriously unpredictable. Moreover, a more satisfactory – in the sense of more ethical – reading of Matthew 23 might be one that challenges its historically one-sided view of the Pharisees as 'hypocrites' and its anti-Semitic potential. Indeed, some reader-focused interpreters are uneasy with the notion that the text itself is capable of *meaning* something. For such readers, texts are inanimate objects, which cannot mean anything by themselves. Nor are they treasure chests containing meaning which is waiting to be discovered. Rather it is in the act of reading by a human reader that meaning emerges. The original New Testament was a collection of Greek letters, which to most English speakers would appear a collection of unintelligible squiggles. Even in English translation, it is in the act of reading – of making sense verbally of the translated letters, words and sentences, of punctuation and intonation – that meaning is created.

However, many scholars are unhappy with this notion that texts themselves do not convey meaning, or provide some constraints on interpretation. After all, we frequently say 'that was a good film', or 'that was a funny film', or 'that was a scary book'. Of course, we are not speaking literally: books or television programmes in themselves are not scary or friendly; films are not moral agents, such that they can be good or bad. What we mean, however, is that books, films and television programmes contain certain potential in them, and are meant to elicit particular responses. That doesn't rule out the possibility that some viewers might find the film a disappointment, or the horror novel tame and hopelessly funny. But it is a claim that readers are not at liberty to do whatever they want with a given text.[6]

What this discussion does suggest (as Bill Countryman's alternative model suggests) is that texts and readers (and indeed authors) cannot be neatly separated. Rather, it is in the dynamic interplay between the two (or three), with and across particular reading communities, that meaning is to be found. Texts elicit particular responses from readers, and urge certain constraints upon readers. However, readers can also challenge texts and the assumptions underlying texts, ask new questions of texts, and open up unexplored aspects to texts. Moreover, a reader's cultural heritage, religious tradition, gender, sexual orientation and educational background will affect (both positively and negatively) what he or she brings to the text, or expects to find in the text. Somewhere in the dialectic between text and reader, meanings emerge, or are discovered, refined and sometimes enlarged.

Reflection

What aspects of who I am, my identity, background, and presuppositions, do I bring to my study of the New Testament? How might these hinder my reading? How might these help? What other voices do I need to listen to?

Can Meanings Change?

One question that is very much on the agenda of contemporary New Testament scholarship is whether the meaning of a text can change. Though not unrelated, this is a different question to the one we have been considering:

Where is meaning to be found? We have seen different answers to this second question: in the intention of the author; in the text itself; in the multiplicity of readers who encounter the text; in the dynamic interplay between all three, within a particular community or set of communities. The question of whether meanings can change is posed particularly today by those who study the reception history of New Testament texts (something of a growth area in biblical scholarship).[7]

Two examples will suffice to illustrate the issue (reception history will be explored in greater depth in Chapter 11). The first is one that spans the Old and New Testaments. When describing the unusual conception of Jesus, Matthew cites from the prophet Isaiah to show how this event fulfils God's will:

> Look, the virgin shall conceive and bear a son . . . (Matthew 1.23, quoting Isaiah 7.14)

The problem is that in the original Hebrew of Isaiah, the word translated here as 'virgin' is better translated as 'young woman'. For it to 'fit' the case of Jesus, Matthew is dependent upon the Greek Septuagint (LXX). Moreover, Old Testament scholars tell us that, from a historical perspective, Isaiah's prophecy almost certainly alluded to the birth of Hezekiah, later king of Judah, rather than to Jesus who was born some 700 years after Isaiah's time.

If meaning is equivalent to the original author's (namely Isaiah's) intention, then Matthew's use is incorrect (the complication here is that we have two 'original authors', Isaiah and Matthew reusing Isaiah in the Greek). But if texts have the capacity to mean more than the original author's conscious intention, then might Matthew's rereading be legitimate? Even if the likely meaning for Isaiah is somehow determinative, it is possible to see what Matthew does as an appropriate, though new reading. A text originally referring to one born to be king (Hezekiah) now finds new resonances centuries later in another believed by his followers to be the final 'King of the Jews'.

The second example is the portrayal of the prostitute 'Babylon' in the book of Revelation (Revelation 17—18). Since the later Middle Ages, and most especially since the Reformation, Revelation's Babylon has sometimes been interpreted as the institution of the papacy, or as individual popes.[8] Yet John's first audiences would most likely have understood the vision to apply to imperial Rome of their own day, not papal Rome of the dim and distant future. To interpret Revelation's Babylon as the Bishop of Rome is surely to do violence to the text. Yet although this is clearly not how John would have understood his vision (and it causes my Catholic hackles to rise!), it may be a legitimate, though secondary, reading. The description of Babylon in Revelation 17 has close echoes of John's description of a Christian prophetess in the church of Thyatira (whom John nicknames 'Jezebel', Revelation 2.20). The link within the text is a reminder to those in the churches of how easy it is for Christians to be associated with 'Babylon', the idolatrous, oppressive empire. Might it have been legitimate, then, at particular periods in history when particular occupants of the papal throne became especially corrupt, for the face of Babylon to be seen in papal faces, just as the visionary John saw it in the face of a first-century Christian in Thyatira?

Is it True?

One particular question has been bubbling under the surface of all this: Is it true? After all, Christians have for centuries read and honoured these particular writings in the conviction that they proclaim the truth about what God has done in Jesus Christ. Indeed, for Christians this is the truth by which human beings are saved. 'You will know the truth,' says Jesus in John's Gospel, 'and the truth will make you free' (John 8.32). But can it be true, if meaning is so elusive, or if different readers can find different 'truths', or different aspects of truth, in the same texts?

Three things might be said in response to this question. First, we have already suggested that the fluidity of texts, and the capacity of human authors to convey more than they intend, leaves 'space' within the historical particularity of those texts for further meanings to be found. That Jesus of Nazareth is Emmanuel, born to be the ultimate King of the Jews, may be even more true of him than it was of the first beneficiary of Isaiah's prophecy, the eighth-century King Hezekiah.

Second, for those who accept either that the (only partially recoverable) intention of the original author is determinative, or that the text itself places some constraints on interpretation, a text cannot mean anything at all. Some readings are untrue. To say that the slaughtered Lamb of Revelation is the devil, to be rejected by Revelation's readers, is clearly an untrue reading of that book.

Finally, when we ask the question: 'Is it true?' we need to ask what we mean by true. A moment's reflection will clarify that there are in fact a number of different kinds of 'truth', and we muddy the waters when we are not clear as to what kind of truth we are talking about. There are claims to truth which are historical (of the 'did it really happen like this' variety) and those which are theological or philosophical (the claim that Jesus was raised from the dead, or that human beings are fallen and in need of redemption, or that free will exists in our world). Truth may be poetic ('love is patient and kind': love is not literally a person, and so cannot literally exhibit these traits) or more prosaic ('Elizabeth II became Queen in 1952'). There are moral truths ('life is sacred') and there are more personal truth statements ('you are beautiful'). We say things that are metaphorically true ('you're a real brick'), and others that are literally so ('The 12.40 train to Reading is usually late'). So too when it comes to reading, and responding to, the New Testament. There are a host of differing truth claims made within it, and for it by others. Some awareness of what those different kinds of truth are will certainly clarify the waters, and help us appreciate more clearly the different kinds of strategy that readers of these diverse writings employ in the service of the truth.

Further Reading

L. William Countryman, 2003, *Interpreting the Truth: Changing the Paradigm of Biblical Studies*, Harrisburg, London and New York: Trinity Press International.

John M. Court, 1997, *Reading the New Testament*, New Testament Readings; London: Routledge.

Joel B. Green (ed.), 1995, *Hearing the New Testament: Strategies for Interpretation*, Grand Rapids, Michigan: Eerdmans.

Mark Allan Powell, 2001, *Chasing the Eastern Star: Adventures in Biblical Reader-Response Criticism*, Louisville, Kentucky: Westminster John Knox Press.

To do

Here are some passages from the New Testament. In each case, ask yourself what kind of truth is implied:

- 'You are the light of the world. A city built on a hill cannot be hidden' (Matthew 5.14).
- 'In those days Jesus came from Nazareth of Galilee and was baptized by John in the Jordan' (Mark 1.9).
- 'In the beginning was the Word, and the Word was with God, and the Word was God' (John 1.1).
- 'But sin, seizing an opportunity in the commandment, produced in me all kinds of covetousness' (Romans 7.8).
- 'Erastus remained in Corinth; Trophimus I left ill in Miletus' (2 Timothy 4.20).
- 'By faith the walls of Jericho fell after they had been encircled for seven days' (Hebrews 11.30).
- 'But you have come to Mount Zion and to the city of the living God, the heavenly Jerusalem, and to innumerable angels in festal gathering' (Hebrews 12.22).
- 'We came in sight of Cyprus; and leaving it on our left, we sailed to Syria and landed at Tyre, because the ship was to unload its cargo there' (Acts 21.3).
- 'For the Lord's sake accept the authority of every human institution, whether of the emperor as supreme, or of governors, as sent by him to punish those who do wrong and to praise those who do right' (1 Peter 2.13–14).
- 'To our God and Father be glory forever and ever. Amen' (Philippians 4.20).
- 'See what love the Father has given us, that we should be called children of God; and that is what we are' (1 John 3.1).
- 'And the one seated there looks like jasper and carnelian, and around the throne is a rainbow that looks like an emerald' (Revelation 4.3).

3

The Jesus Effect

The Beginnings of the Jesus Tradition

One of the most creative works of New Testament scholarship in recent years is the novel *The Shadow of the Galilean* by the influential German scholar Gerd Theissen.[9] Subtitled 'the quest of the historical Jesus in narrative form', it presents itself as the autobiographical account of a Palestinian Jew living in the first decades of the first century CE. Although a direct contemporary of Jesus, the narrator Andreas of Sepphoris (a prominent Galilean city close to Jesus' home village of Nazareth) never actually meets him face to face. Indeed, his first and only direct sight of Jesus is when the latter hangs dead on a cross outside Jerusalem.

That does not mean that Andreas is oblivious to Jesus, however. On the contrary, wherever he goes, he is brought face to face with the impact of Jesus on those who did encounter him directly. As he travels from village to farm to small Galilean town, and even to the great city of Jerusalem to the south, he encounters the effects of Jesus' presence, Jesus' teaching and Jesus' activity. A sick little girl longs for Jesus to come and heal her, just as she has heard stories about Jesus healing others. A meal outside a roadside customs house (recently deserted by a certain Levi, who had left at a moment's notice to follow this Jesus) is interrupted by a strange array of the sick, poor and dispossessed, coming to claim their rights as citizens of the kingdom of God. Gathered round the table or the fire in the evening, people recount their own reminiscences of Jesus, and often disagree vehemently with one another as to what precisely he meant and how they should respond.

Theissen's novel is a highly imaginative, sophisticated account of how we gain access to the Jesus who walked the roads of first-century Galilee. The scholarly attempt to do so – the so-called 'quest of the historical Jesus' – is explored further in Chapter 2 of the companion volume to this, *SCM Study-guide to the Books of the New Testament*. I mention Theissen's book here not only because it conveys vividly the socially destabilizing nature of Jesus' kingdom preaching (people leaving jobs, homes and families; the disenfranchised and marginalized being brought into the centre of things). It is particularly relevant for this chapter because of the highly plausible historical portrait it paints of how 'the Jesus tradition' might have emerged.

'The Jesus tradition' is the scholarly shorthand for the interpreted memory, passed from one generation to another, of what Jesus said and did. The bulk of this in the New Testament is to be found in the four gospels (for example, miracles and exorcisms, conflict stories, parables and aphorisms that Jesus told, his teaching about the kingdom of God), although some traditions are also found in the letters (for example, what Jesus did at his last supper with his disciples or his teaching about divorce). What *The Shadow of the Galilean* makes clear is that, from the beginning, Jesus was known primarily by his effects. The tradition about Jesus' deeds and actions emerged out of the multifaceted experience of Jesus, told and retold orally before it was written down, and continuing to be retold orally after it had been written down. Jesus had an impact on people, from the start, in many different ways. The Jesus tradition reflects the community's attempt (or diverse communities' attempts) to perpetuate that impact, and continue to reflect on its meaning for later generations of Christians.

Fact and Interpretation

This recognition is important, because New Testament scholars have often tended to write as though one can separate out original 'facts' from the later 'interpretation' which the Church has laid over them. Strip away that later theological, dogmatic interpretation, and we will be left with the bare facts which can be interpreted differently. The 'quest of the historical Jesus' often proceeds from precisely that presupposition. In extreme cases, quite extravagant claims are made. Many of us will have seen, while browsing the shelves of W.H. Smith or Dillon's at a railway station or airport, the kind of sensationalist book which claims to give us 'the real Jesus', hidden by the churches for centuries, but now brought into the clear light of day. But even serious, mainstream scholars often draw a dichotomy between 'bare facts' and 'later interpretation' in the Jesus tradition.

What they are wanting to affirm, of course, is an important truth. The early Christians interpreted the tradition about Jesus. The fact that we possess three gospels (Matthew, Mark and Luke) which are almost certainly related at a literary level, enables us to see how earlier written material is reshaped and newer interpretations given to it. Take, for example, the three synoptic accounts of Jesus' baptism (opposite).

Most scholars think that Mark's account is the earliest of the three, and the main source for the other two. The following observations can be made from the three accounts, which point to a process of subsequent reflection on the tradition:

- Mark clearly sees the baptism as a crucial event in preparation for Jesus' ministry (along with the temptation story which immediately follows). He focuses on the effect on Jesus himself: his seeing the heavens 'torn apart' (compare the 'tearing apart' of the temple curtain on Jesus' death: Mark 15.38), and his hearing the voice declaring him to be God's Son.
- Matthew appears decidedly embarrassed or bewildered by the event, for it seems to suggest that John (who baptizes) is superior to Jesus (who is baptized). He includes a dialogue between John and Jesus to explain why the baptism was necessary ('to fulfil all righteousness').
- Matthew also changes the words of the heavenly voice. For him, the purpose of this divine disclosure is not to reveal to Jesus his own identity (are we to presume that Matthew thinks Jesus knows it already?), but to make it known publicly. Jesus' divine sonship is not to be hidden, but to be proclaimed to all who will hear.
- Luke also appears somewhat embarrassed by the suggestion that Jesus was baptized by John the Baptist, Jesus' inferior. He deals with it somewhat differently, however. By mentioning John's arrest by Herod Antipas in the preceding verses (Luke 3.19–20), he thereby removes him visibly from the scene. The result is that we are not told explicitly who baptized either Jesus or 'all the people'.

THE JESUS EFFECT 43

Matthew 3.13–17	Mark 1.9–11	Luke 3.21–2
Then Jesus came from Galilee to John at the Jordan, to be baptized by him. *John would have prevented him, saying, 'I need to be baptized by you, and do you come to me?' But Jesus answered him, 'Let it be so now; for it is proper for us in this way to fulfil all righteousness.' Then he consented.*	In those days Jesus came from Nazareth of Galilee	Now when *all the people were baptized,*
And when Jesus had been baptized, just as he came up from the water, suddenly the heavens were opened to him and he saw the Spirit of God descending like a dove and alighting on him.	and was baptized by John in the Jordan. And just as he was coming up out of the water, he saw the heavens torn apart and the Spirit descending like a dove on him.	and when Jesus also had been baptized *and was praying,* the heaven was opened, and the Holy Spirit descended upon him *in bodily form* like a dove.
And a voice from heaven said, 'This is my Son, the Beloved, *with whom* I am well pleased.'	And a voice came from heaven, 'You are my Son, the Beloved; with you I am well pleased.'	And a voice came from heaven, 'You are my Son, the Beloved; with you I am well pleased.'

- By the addition of one phrase 'and was praying', Luke interprets this event as one of those key moments of intimacy between Jesus and his Father which results in decisive action. Throughout his Gospel, Jesus is presented as praying at key moments in his ministry (for example, before choosing the twelve, on the mountain of transfiguration, in Gethsemane).

- Finally, Luke offers clarification of an ambiguous phrase in Mark's account. Mark describes how the Spirit descended 'like a dove' onto Jesus. But does this mean, metaphorically, that the Spirit swooped down like a dove or some other bird might be expected to? Or did the Spirit manifest itself in the appearance of the dove? Matthew's 'and alighting on him' might be an attempt to suggest the former. Luke's 'in bodily form' is an unambiguous statement of the latter.

Clearly, the individual evangelists (gospel writers) are interpreting the event in the light of questions which emerge for them. Where they locate the event in their overall story of Jesus, the imagery they use which evokes particular ideas or events (for example, the Spirit hovering at creation came to be associated with a dove in Jewish tradition), and their reworking of their sources, is all part of the process of interpretation.

But New Testament scholars have often been too swift to move from this obvious evidence for ongoing interpretation to suggesting that such interpretation *only* occurs at a secondary stage. Yet how likely is this? Would not the event of Jesus' baptism have been interpreted in particular ways from the start, by those who witnessed it (for example, Jesus himself; John the Baptist)? That does not *necessarily* require us to accept that the more 'spectacular' visible signs, such as heavens being ripped apart, or audible heavenly voices, were part of the interpretation from the start (it may or may not have been a more 'interior' experience for Jesus). These may reflect a deepening theological reflection upon the event at a later stage. But to suggest that interpretation of this event *only* began at a later stage is surely naïve. Indeed, the baptism of John already had a certain meaning, or set of meanings, prior to Jesus' own baptism (a call to Israel to return to its roots; a washing 'for forgiveness of sins').

Or consider first-century witnesses to the crucifixion of Jesus. What would they have made of what they saw? Of course, there are certain bare facts: Jesus was being executed by crucifixion; the Romans were the executioners; it took place outside the city walls. But what did the individual witnesses see? A Roman might have seen a common criminal (one among many), perhaps a slave or a rebel against the Roman state (various crimes for which cruci-fixion was the punishment). Another might conclude, as a result of hearsay or Jesus' reputation, that he was unjustly condemned. Unlike the Roman, a Jewish observer would naturally attempt to make sense of this dying figure in terms provided by the Hebrew scriptures. These writings, after all, pro-vided the lens through which Jews saw and made sense of reality.

Not all would come to the same conclusion, however. Was he a false prophet who led Israel astray (the fact that he was 'hanging on a tree' may suggest he was cursed by God: Deuteronomy 21.23; Galatians 3.13)? A true prophet, suffering for the people? A martyr? A righteous person enduring unjust treatment by his enemies? These questions would surely have arisen from the start, even if there were no immediate answers to such questions. None of the accounts of what these Jewish bystanders saw would have been an 'uninterpreted' statement of 'bare fact'. This recognition does not contra-dict the clear New Testament evidence that the early Christians continued to reflect on the Old Testament scriptures in order to make sense of the un-expected suffering and brutal death of Jesus. A comparison of the gospel passion narratives will show the extent to which the language and imagery of the Old Testament continued to shape and influence the Christian story of Jesus' passion. That is not disputed, even though scholars debate vehemently the precise relationship between scripture and history in these narratives.[10] The point here is simply that attempts to make sense of Jesus' passion in the light of the Old Testament would not have *begun* with later, theological speculation. Rather they would have been there from the beginning.

Reflection

Recall a scenario you have witnessed recently (along with other people). How did you interpret it? Was it interpreted in the same way by others? How did you differ? Did you change your interpreta-tion after listening to others? Can you distinguish any 'bare facts' from the interpretation of those facts?

Oral or Literary?

Our example of the baptism of Jesus is a literary example. We possess three overlapping accounts which agree so much in wording and content that there is almost certainly some literary relationship between them. The common scholarly thesis (reflected in our analysis) is that both Matthew and Luke have used Mark as their main source for this story, and reinterpreted Mark's account in line with their own particular understanding and questions. Detailed differences, as well as wider literary context (where an author locates a particular story or teaching, which may differ from its context in another gospel), can be examined to shed light on the meaning of the texts. Such literary analysis remains important for our study of the gospels, especially the synoptics.

Nevertheless, what has been said so far reminds us that the tradition about Jesus has an oral as well as a literary dimension. That is, the effect of Jesus, his person and his teaching, was recounted by those who felt it by word of mouth, even before it came to be written down. Indeed, the second-century Bishop Papias of Hierapolis (c.60–130) continued to prize the 'living and abiding voice' of the oral tradition alongside that of the written gospels.

Scholars continue to debate whether we should envisage the traditions now preserved in the written gospels as primarily oral or written. Given that we only possess the finished literary documents, isolating their sources, and distinguishing oral from literary, is not at all easy. That Christianity could produce literary texts prior to the gospels is evident from the letters of Paul, the earliest of which date from approximately 20 years after Jesus' death. However, widespread illiteracy in the ancient world may have meant that many of the stories about Jesus were circulated and shaped orally in the period between Jesus and the writing of the gospels. Was the story of Jesus' passion written down prior to Mark, or were standardized versions of it retold orally? What about the blocks of miracle stories, or conflict stories, or parables, found in Mark's Gospel? Are they in blocks because they were already grouped together prior to Mark, and if so, were they in written form or grouped together in the oral retelling? Perhaps we should not push the distinctions too far. Luke Timothy Johnson reminds us of the extent to which 'oral' and 'literary' overlapped in the ancient world.[11] Rabbis who debated orally could also make written notes of those debates; speeches were carefully crafted in written form before being delivered orally. A modern parallel would be collections of published sermons by noted Church leaders or preachers, originally delivered before congregations.

Nevertheless, a recent criticism by James Dunn and others is that the essentially *literary* nature of the New Testament has prevented scholars from recognizing the full implications of early Christianity's essentially *oral* context.[12] Dunn sketches out what some of these implications might be:

- Oral tradition is something to be *performed*, and people remember what was heard (rather than going back to check the details against a written text). Indeed, even literary texts like the letters of Paul or the book of Revelation would have been received orally, performed by a reader and heard by the congregation.
- Oral tradition is a community's tradition rather than primarily individual reminiscence: it is honed in the shared experience, reflection and correction of the community (originally, perhaps, in evening gatherings in Galilean villages, though increasingly in the liturgical assemblies of the early Christians). Christian communities would have had a store of tradition from which individual 'performances', or individual texts would have drawn, and it could be presumed that Christian audiences would have picked up allusions to aspects of that store.
- In oral societies, recognized figures have a key role in 'performing' the tradition and ensuring that the tradition is preserved (Dunn lists singers of tales, bards, elders, teachers and rabbis). For the early Christians, the apostles and other authoritative teachers would have exercised this role (indeed, Acts 2.42 refers to the 'teaching of the apostles'). Nor would this have been fragmentary: grouping of similar material is likely to have occurred from the earliest time.
- In oral tradition, there is no 'original version', which is then interpreted ('corrupted') by later generations. Rather, there are likely to be several 'versions' from the start, all interpretations of the original 'impulse' or the 'Jesus effect'. While in our gospels we can detect earlier *literary* sources, which have been reinterpreted by later authors (for example, Matthew's expanded version of Mark's baptism story), at the *oral* stage there would not have been just one 'authentic' version.

- Oral tradition tends to combine *stability* with *flexibility*: every oral per-formance is a fresh performance; the tradition is retold not simply to keep hearers in continuity with the past, but also to address the present and future.

Something of this complex interplay between literary and oral has left its mark on the New Testament, especially the gospels, and will need to be taken into account in interpretation. Often, differences between gospel accounts (as in the baptism) seem to be due to redaction at the literary stage. Mark is used by Matthew and Luke (or, in some scenarios, Matthew is used by Mark and Luke). However, there may be occasions – when the parallels are looser – when parallel oral versions of the same saying or deed are being used by individual evangelists.

To do

Look at the following parallel passages: Matthew 8.1–4 and parallels; Matthew 14.22–33 and parallels; Matthew 17.14–18 and parallels. If you have a synopsis of the gospels, this will make your task easier. Which examples seem to presuppose a literary relation-ship (for example, Mark being source for Matthew and or Luke, or vice versa)? Are there any which might suggest use of oral tradi-tion, in which similar but parallel versions of the same event can be passed on?

The Lens of Easter

One further factor needs to be taken into account in understanding the New Testament writings as witness to the Jesus effect (or the 'impact of Jesus' as Dunn prefers to call it). That is the claim that Jesus had been raised from the dead after death. What distinguishes the New Testament writings from non-Christian writings of the period is their proclamation of Christian faith in Jesus as Lord. But this proclamation is not simply one that emerged dur-ing Jesus' ministry. Rather, the evidence suggests that it was only after the first Easter that Christians came to see that Jesus of Nazareth was not simply a teacher, or prophet, or healer, but the one in whom God had definitively acted. Consider the following quotations from the New Testament:

• Therefore let the entire house of Israel know with certainty that God has made him both Lord and Messiah, this Jesus whom you crucified (Acts 2.36).
• the gospel concerning his Son, who was descended from David according to the flesh, and was declared to be Son of God with power according to the spirit of holiness by resurrection from the dead, Jesus Christ our Lord ... (Romans 1.3–4).
• he humbled himself and became obedient to the point of death – even death on a cross. Therefore God also highly exalted him and gave him the name that is above every name ... (Philippians 2.8–9).
• When he had made purification for sins, he sat down at the right hand of the Majesty on high, having become as much superior to angels as the name he has inherited is more excellent than theirs (Hebrews 1.3b–4).

What seems to underlie all these passages (even though they differ in their overall Christology) is that it was only in the light of what happened to Jesus after death that the early Christians came to see who he really is. In the light of Easter, they came to address him differently: as 'Lord' (that is, sharing God's Name YHWH, 'the name that is above every name'), Son and Messiah.

So the gospels are not simply varied accounts of how Jesus was remembered during his ministry. Rather, all are written a considerable period after his death, expressing the conviction that Jesus of Nazareth is also the risen Lord; that the crucified one is also the living one. They tell the story, as it were, through resurrection-tinted lenses. They are documents of faith, and that Easter faith permeates the whole, to varying degrees, even if the story of Jesus' resurrection – or rather of the effects of Jesus' resurrection on his disciples – is not told until the end of the story. Two examples will serve to illustrate this:

Example 1: Read the account of the Walking on the Water in Mark 6.47–52 and Matthew 14.22–33. How do the two versions of the story end? Why might Matthew's ending be surprising, in the light of, for example, Romans 1.3–4 above? What post-Easter context might have shaped Matthew's version?

Example 2: Read John's account of the so-called 'Cleansing of the Temple' (John 2.13–22; you might wish to look briefly at the parallel accounts in Matthew 21.12–17; Mark 11.15–19; Luke 19.45–8). Pay attention especially to John's explanation of this event's meaning in verses 21–2. What does this suggest about the role of the resurrection in understanding the significance of Jesus' pre-Easter actions?

In both examples, the resurrection forces the evangelists to view an event in the ministry of Jesus in a new light, and to view the pre-Easter Jesus in a new light. What we find happening in the gospels are particular instances of a wider phenomenon going on throughout the New Testament. Although it was the experience of the resurrection which 'opened the eyes' of the disciples to Jesus' role and identity, forcing them to see him in a new way, it provoked a further question. If Jesus is now Lord or Son of God, was he not so before? Did Jesus' status simply change when he was raised from the dead, or was how we now see him already true of him during his earthly life? One can see, in the gospels and other New Testament writings, particular earlier (as well as later) moments being isolated as crucial points at which Jesus' unique relationship with God is highlighted or revealed (Raymond Brown calls these 'christological moments').[13]

Worship and Experience

When did the early Christians retell and re-enact the Jesus tradition? When, moreover, did they confess Jesus as Lord and Son? They did so in their preaching to fellow Jews and to pagans, in their teaching to new converts, but especially in the context of worship. This context has left a very strong mark on the New Testament writings.

We are helped here by the fact that liturgy (the structured worship of religious communities) tends to be conservative, and often preserves prayers

---

Table 3: 'Christological Moments'.

- The Parousia (when Christ returns as Son of Man): e.g.
  1 Corinthians 16.22; 1 Thessalonians 1.10
- The Resurrection and Exaltation: e.g. Acts 2.33–6; Romans
  1.3–4
- Jesus' Baptism: preserved in the synoptics
- Jesus' Infancy: e.g. Luke 2.41–51; Infancy Gospel of Thomas
- Jesus' Conception: Matthew 1; Luke 1
- Pre-existence: John 1; Hebrews 1; possibly Philippians 2.6–11

---

and invocations in other languages. The liturgies of many English-speaking Christians preserve elements of Hebrew (for example, Alleluia; Amen) and Greek (for example, Kyrie eleison). Both Catholic and Anglican churches often sing parts of the Eucharist in Latin (for example, the 'Gloria', 'Credo', 'Sanctus' and 'Agnus Dei'), even when the bulk of the service is in the vernacular. More widespread in Anglicanism is the practice of using Latin titles for the New Testament canticles at Matins and Evensong (the Benedictus, Magnificat and Nunc Dimittis), despite the fact that they are sung or said in English.

This same phenomenon can be found within the New Testament. The Hebrew 'Amen' and 'Alleluia' occur in contexts that suggest prayer, hymnody and other fragments of liturgy (for example, Romans 9.5; 16.27; 1 Corinthians 14.16; Revelation 1.7; 19.1–8). But there are also echoes of prayer in Aramaic, Jesus' probable mother tongue. Jesus himself is recorded as praying to God as 'Abba' (an intimate form for 'father', Mark 14.36), while Paul attests that Christians also addressed God this way in prayer, under the inspiration of the Holy Spirit (Romans 8.15; Galatians 4.6). Another Aramaic prayer, 'Maranatha' (probably meaning 'Our Lord, come!') is preserved at 1 Corinthians 16.22, and translated into Greek at Revelation 22.20. Moreover, there are a significant number of hymns and canticles cited in texts like Luke and Revelation, and fragments of hymns and creeds embedded in Paul's letters. Above all, we have two versions of the Lord's Prayer preserved in the gospels (Matthew 6.9–13; Luke 11.2–4, perhaps reflecting the different liturgical forms of different churches), as well as variant accounts of Jesus' words over the bread and cup at the last supper, re-enacted ritually by Christians during the Lord's Supper or Eucharist (Matthew 26.26–9; Mark 14.22–5; Luke 22.14–23; 1 Corinthians 11.23–6). All these are indications that, underlying and prior to the writing of these books, Christians prayed, sang and worshipped. The New Testament is a window providing glimpses of this praying, worshipping Church.

To do

See if you can locate the excerpts of early Christian liturgy in the following New Testament passages. Try to identify the different types (for example, hymns; creeds (statements of faith); prayers; doxologies (prayers of praise)):

- John 1.1–18
- Romans 16.25–7
- 1 Corinthians 8.1–6
- 1 Corinthians 15.1–11
- Philippians 2.1–13
- Ephesians 1.15–23
- 1 Timothy 3.14–16
- Jude 24–5
- Revelation 4.9–11

One of the most striking features of those fragments of early liturgy in the New Testament, is the centrality they give to Jesus. Devotion to Jesus, along with that to Israel's God, is expressed there in hymns, in credal statements, and in titles ascribed to him (as in the confession that 'Jesus is Lord!' 1 Corinthians 12.3). Indeed, in certain of these expressions of devotion, Jesus is the object of worship. In Revelation, for example, while John is twice expressly forbidden to worship an angel (Revelation 19.10; 22.8–9), there is no such restriction on the worship of Jesus the Lamb.

Scholars debate how early such devotion to Christ developed. For some (for example, Maurice Casey), it was a secondary and evolutionary development, traceable to Christianity's movement from a purely Jewish into a wider pagan environment. For others (for example, Christopher Rowland;

Larry Hurtado), its roots are traceable to Christianity's original Jewish context, although they differ as to whether it was a unique development (a quick 'explosion') or has antecedents in Jewish traditions about divine attributes (such as the Word or Wisdom), privileged human beings (such as Moses and Enoch), or principal angels (such as Michael, Yahoel or Metatron).[14] Whether or not there were precise antecedents, Hurtado and others have made a good case for devotion to and worship of Jesus being a feature of the Christian movement from its earliest Jewish stage. When they came together, they proclaimed Jesus as Lord (Aramaic *mare*; Greek *Kurios*), they celebrated his presence in their eucharistic assemblies, and they awaited his return in glory. They experienced Jesus as exalted Lord, and found themselves celebrating this fact in their worship. Their articulation of Christology, one feels, constrained by Jewish monotheism, is struggling to catch up with their experience.

Rereading Israel's Scriptures

Our consideration of the 'Jesus effect' would be incomplete without some reflection upon early Christian use of the Old Testament. Our discussion above of possible reactions to the crucifixion of Jesus highlights the way in which, post-Easter, the Jewish followers of Jesus found themselves rereading Israel's scriptures. It is important to note the emphasis upon *re*reading. Later Christians have often read Old Testament quotations in the New as if they were clear-cut prophecies of the coming Messiah (from the Hebrew word meaning 'anointed'), portraying a kind of Identikit picture of the Messiah which all Jews would instantly have recognized, and to which Jesus conformed perfectly. This makes the relative failure of the Christian message among fellow Jews all the more puzzling. The anti-Semitic potential in such a position is obvious: the Jews must have been disobedient, or deliberately obstructive, or bewilderingly obtuse.

The truth seems to be, however, that the early Christians were not simply reading the Old Testament scriptures in the same way as their contemporaries. Rather they were forced to reread them in unexpected ways. First, there seems to have been great diversity in Jewish 'messianic' expectation (that is, expectation of an anointed figure who in the last days would act on God's behalf: see Table 4). Indeed, many Jews may not have been waiting for a particular Messiah at all. More significantly, prior to Jesus there does not seem to have been an expectation of a suffering and dying Messiah. Their conviction that Jesus was Israel's Messiah (confirmed by God raising him from death) forced his followers to go back to the scriptures, and read them anew in the light of Jesus, and especially of his unexpected passion and crucifixion.

In other words, the early Christians not only looked again at passages already understood as prophecies of a coming Messiah. They also looked elsewhere in scripture to passages not hitherto thought to be about a Messiah, and read such non-messianic passages messianically. To make sense of Jesus' suffering, they turned to a strange set of poems about a 'suffering servant' in Isaiah (for example, Isaiah 42.1–4; 52.13—53.12), who bore the sins of many and was exalted after his humiliation, and psalms that envisaged the suffering of the righteous Israelite (for example, Psalms 22; 69). They discovered passages such as Zechariah 9.9, which spoke of a humble king riding on an ass rather than a bold military warrior. They found in Psalm 110, probably originally used for the coronation of Israel's king, a passage which reflected their conviction that the risen Jesus had been exalted to God's right hand. The rich potential in the 'deep well' of Israel's scriptures was exploited to the full in the early Christian re-imagining of the tradition in the light of Christ. Their procedure was that which Luke attributes to the risen Lord towards the end of his gospel account: 'Then beginning with Moses and all the prophets, he interpreted to them the things about himself in all the scriptures' (Luke 24.27).

To the modern mind, all this might look like a case of special pleading. In the context of ancient Jewish methods of scriptural exegesis, however, their quite creative manner of rereading scripture would not have been considered surprising, even if their particular conclusions were decidedly controversial. But it is yet another example of the powerful 'Jesus effect' which turned many first-century Jewish communities upside down. The New Testament writings, and the traditions and experiences they convey, are testimony to that explosion. The next few chapters will focus upon a number of scholarly reading strategies for approaching these writings in detail.

Table 4: Examples of Jewish messianic expectations.

- Heavenly figure (for example, Michael)
- Prophet like Moses
- Returned Elijah
- Warrior king of David's line
- Peaceable king
- Priest Messiah and royal Messiah

Further Reading

James D. G. Dunn, 2005, *A New Perspective on Jesus: What the Quest for the Historical Jesus Missed*, London: SPCK.

Larry W. Hurtado, 2005, *How on Earth Did Jesus Become a God?* Grand Rapids, Michigan/Cambridge: Eerdmans.

Luke Timothy Johnson, 1999, *The Writings of the New Testament: An Interpretation*, rev. edition, London: SCM Press, pp. 125–58.

Gerd Theissen, 1987, *The Shadow of the Galilean*, ET London: SCM Press.

4

Determining the Text

Relearning How to Read

Imagine being asked to read the beginning of the Gospel according to Mark, and being presented with the following text (a rough approximation of what the opening of an ancient copy of Mark's Gospel would have looked like):

ΑΡΧΗΤΟΥΕΥΑΓΓΕΛΙΟΥΙΗΣ
ΟΥΧΡΙΣΤΟΥΥΙΟΥΘΕΟΥΚΑΘ
ΩΣΓΕΓΡΑΠΤΑΙΕΝΤΩΗΣΑΙΑ
ΤΩΠΡΟΦΗΤΗΙΔΟΥΑΠΟΣΤΕΛ
ΛΩΤΟΝΑΓΓΕΛΟΝΜΟΥΠΡΟΠ
ΡΟΣΩΠΟΥΣΟΥΟΣΚΑΤΑΣΚΕΥ
ΑΣΕΙΤΗΝΟΔΟΝΣΟΥΦΩΝΗΒΟ
ΩΝΤΟΣΕΝΤΗΕΡΗΜΩΕΤΟΙΜ

You would be understandably puzzled to be handed this, rather than a nicely bound copy of a modern English translation, especially if you had not taken a course in New Testament Greek. But even if you were a Greek scholar, you would realize that what was being asked of you was something rather different from our modern concept of 'reading the New Testament':

- The text you have been given was originally composed in an ancient foreign language, not in your native tongue. Though we often know theoretically that the New Testament was first written in an ancient form of Greek, it can still be a shock to be reminded of it in practice.

- This passage is going to require some careful preparation if you are to read it intelligently, given that it is written in capitals, with no punctuation and no spaces between words. It is a reminder that the role of the reader in the early Church was an important and complex one.
- The request to 'read' means something rather different when dealing with an ancient Greek manuscript than with a modern English translation, read in a modern Western mind-set. Ancient 'readers' asked to read a Greek text such as this would not have understood the relatively modern concept of reading silently, nor would they have regarded reading as a primarily individual activity. Rather, the ancient reader would have read or performed a text out loud to a group. Revelation 1.3, for example, envisages that this is how the book of Revelation would be received: 'Blessed is the one who reads aloud the words of the prophecy, and blessed are those who hear and who keep what is written in it; for the time is near'. The same goes for the letters of Paul (for example, Colossians 4.16), and probably also for the gospels (for example, Mark 13.14).

In other words, we should not underestimate the 'strangeness' of the New Testament writings. They were written in an ancient form of a foreign language, the product of a different time and a different culture, and were received through an aural rather than visual form of reading (with the very different effects that entails). Any attempt at translation, though necessary, is inevitably a process of interpretation. So too is an attempt – equally necessary – to bridge the gap between that ancient culture and our very different cultural norms and expectations. The word is strange, and we should not be tempted to jump too swiftly from that strangeness.

What is the Original Text?

But before we attempt to interpret – and even the act of reading, with its making sense of words and sentence structure, and addition of punctuation and intonation, is an act of interpretation – we need a text to start with. This raises the prior question: what is the original text of the New Testament? As we saw in Chapter 1, one of the consequences of the 'human aspect' of the

New Testament is that there are a huge number of variations between the ancient manuscripts. We do not possess any 'autograph' copies of any New Testament book (that is, the version which came from the hand of the original author), only copies of copies, or better, copies of copies of copies. More than 5,000 manuscripts containing sections of, or the whole New Testament exist in Greek alone, dating from the second to the sixteenth centuries. Another 10,000 survive in Latin, while there are also translations in languages such as Syriac, Coptic and Armenian.

The Greek manuscripts fall into two main categories: continuous text manuscripts (like our published New Testaments, where whole books are given in sequence), and lectionaries (where selected passages are arranged for liturgical use, providing appropriate readings for the liturgical year and particular feasts in it). Some of the earliest continuous text manuscripts (largely fragments) are written on papyrus (in shorthand, designated by P + a number). Most, however, are on parchment. These parchment texts can be further divided into:

- Uncials or majuscules (that is, written in capital letters, often without breaks between words); these are variously designated by a Greek, Roman or Hebrew capital letter, or a number beginning with zero. Among the uncials are the most famous Greek codices: the fourth-century Codex Sinaiticus (known as ℵ or 01) and Codex Vaticanus (B or 03), the fifth-century Codex Alexandrinus (A or 02), and the bilingual Greek–Latin Codex Bezae (D or 04).
- Cursives or minuscules (written in cursive script, which tended to replace uncials from about the ninth century onwards), numbered from 1 onwards.

These abbreviations are used, for example, in the critical apparatus (the footnotes listing important variant readings) of the two main editions of the Greek New Testament widely used by scholars and theological students: the United Bible Societies' *Greek New Testament* and the Nestle-Aland *Novum Testamentum Graece*. Each of these has a helpful introduction explaining the symbols and their usage.

The fact that, until the invention of printing, writings like the New Testament had to be copied by hand, meant that errors inevitably crept into the text, as well as deliberate changes to received texts. A number of factors were at play here:

- Scribes made mistakes due to visual errors: missing a line, or a phrase, due to the fact that words were repeated in close proximity, or words ended with similar letters. The technical term for this is *homoeoteleuton*, from the Greek meaning 'like ending'. This is one possible explanation for the lack of the words 'son of God [Greek *huiou theou*]' in some manuscripts of Mark 1.1: six of the seven Greek words in this verse end in -*ou*.
- Scribes made mistakes due to errors of hearing: this happened when several scribes were copying manuscripts being read out by another. In Romans 5.1, for example, there is little difference in the pronunciation of the Greek verbs *echōmen* ('Let us have [peace with God]') and *echomen* ('We have . . .'). Either the exhortation or the statement could be the original. A similar reason could account for the variations at Revelation 1.5: has Christ freed us (*lusanti*) from our sins, or washed us (*lousanti*), or called us (*kalesanti*)?
- Scribes made marginal explanatory notes, or raised questions, which a later scribe copied into the main body of the text. A possible example of this is to be found at John 4.9 ('Jews do not share things in common with Samaritans'), which is lacking in a small number of manuscripts, including Codex Bezae and the original hand of (as opposed to later corrections to) Codex Sinaiticus.
- Scribes made deliberate changes to the text in order to harmonize one gospel with another (a reflection of the growing authority of the texts, and a sense that they should 'speak with one voice'). For example, although at Mark 1.8 the vast majority of manuscripts speak of Jesus' coming baptism as 'in the holy Spirit', a small number add 'and fire', harmonizing it with Matthew and Luke.
- Scribes altered what they believed to be a mistake: indeed, this may underlie the tendency to harmonize, out of a conviction that they were restoring an original reading which had become 'corrupted'. One fairly

clear example is Mark 5.1 (and the parallel at Matthew 8.28 and Luke 8.26): some texts have Jesus crossing the Sea of Galilee to the region of the 'Gerasenes'. Those with any knowledge of Middle Eastern geography would know that the city of Gerasa was a long way from the lake (some 37 miles). Some scribes seem to have corrected this to 'Gadarenes', which is better, but still about five miles from the Sea of Galilee. Better still is the variant 'Gergasenes', for Gergasa was on the eastern shore of the lake.

• Scribes deliberately corrected manuscripts for doctrinal reasons, reflecting their own more developed understanding of the Christian faith. This may explain the omission of the words 'nor the Son' from some manuscripts of Matthew 24.36 (see Mark 13.32). These words, implying the Son's ignorance of the timing of the end, may have been understood as undermining Christ's divinity. Similarly, the suggestion that Christ became 'angry' (a minority reading at Mark 1.41) could have been altered to 'moved with pity' for reverential motives.

• Scribes were clarifying an ambiguity in the text, or supplying a perceived lack. An example of the former might be Jude 5, where the ambiguous 'the Lord' (which could be a reference either to the Father or to Jesus) is read in other manuscripts as 'God', 'Jesus' and 'God Christ'. The various versions of the ending of Mark's Gospel may be examples of the latter, supplied by scribes who considered 16.8 an unsatisfactory way to conclude Mark's book.

• 'Free-floating' stories (that is, stories that were considered valuable traditions about Jesus but which were not contained within any particular New Testament book) were copied into New Testament manuscripts by scribes wishing to preserve them for posterity. One example of this is the story of the woman taken in adultery. Although it is generally printed as John 7.53—8.11, this passage lacks the style and vocabulary of John's Gospel, and interrupts the flow of John's narrative. Moreover, some ancient manuscripts include it in other places (after John 7.36, or at the end of John's Gospel; after Luke 21.38, or at the end of Luke's Gospel), while others omit it completely.

> **To do**
>
> Look in your English translation, or if you read Greek your Greek
> New Testament, and select three verses where there are variant
> readings (in English versions, denoted in a footnote by a phrase
> such as 'Other ancient authorities read . . .'). Can you find rea-
> sons to account for a scribe making a mistake here, or deliberately
> changing an earlier reading? (You may find it helpful to consult
> commentaries on these verses, particularly if you cannot read the
> Greek original).

Determining the Original Text

Textual criticism is the name for that branch of New Testament scholarship
that seeks to determine what the original Greek text of the New Testament
is likely to have been.[15] This involves the complex task of comparing and
categorizing the huge number of ancient manuscripts (as opposed to printed
versions of the New Testament) which have survived. In fact, textual critics
engage in a twofold quest:

- to determine the original text of the New Testament writings;
- to explain how the huge number of variant readings may have come
  about.

Comparing the manuscripts is not an easy task. Textual critics have sometimes attempted to group manuscripts together according to 'families', often
positing complex relationships between them, in the manner of a family
tree. The family tree analogy breaks down, however, in that it has not proved
possible to isolate particular texts which are obvious 'ancestors' to later
'offspring'. Many textual critics prefer looser groupings of texts, reflecting
similar mistakes or omitting the same passages: for example, Alexandrian,
Western, Byzantine (particular differences between the Alexandrian and
the Western texts are noticeable in Luke and Acts). In addition, attention

is often given to the geographical origin of manuscripts (for example, Italy, North Africa, Asia Minor, Syria): this helps determine whether specific readings are widespread, or restricted to one particular geographical region.

Two particular issues continue to be hotly debated by textual critics. First, should preference be given to the earliest manuscripts in reconstructing the original text of the New Testament, given that they have had less time to accumulate corruptions? Second, should one give priority to a reading found in a large number of manuscripts over a minority reading found in perhaps one or two? While some would answer in the affirmative, others maintain that one or both positions is flawed. First, the date of a manuscript does not *necessarily* give you the date of a text being followed in that manuscript. A monk in the ninth century may have copied a manuscript from the third century, while a fifth-century scribe may have used a late and corrupt fourth-century manuscript.

Second, a reading found in a large number of manuscripts is not *necessarily* more reliable, because those manuscripts may simply be perpetuating a change made by one earlier scribe. It may be that only one Greek manuscript has preserved the original reading at a particular point. Alternatively, translations in languages other than Greek (for example, Latin, Coptic) may have preserved an original reading not found in any of the surviving Greek manuscripts. Hence these are also appealed to in the critical apparatus of editions of the Greek New Testament.

Criteria for Assessing Variant Readings

How can we go about reconstructing the original text? Besides those external criteria discussed in the previous section, textual critics have developed a number of internal criteria for assessing the variant readings of a given passage:

- A reading that can best account for the emergence of the other readings is likely to be original. For example, if there are three alternative readings, textual critics will ask whether two of them are explicable as corruptions or corrections of the other.

- Readings 'out of character' with the author, or the literary context of the passage, or reflecting a later theological perspective, are likely to be secondary.
- The 'harder reading' (*lectio difficilior*) is generally to be preferred, on the grounds that the scribes will tend to iron out difficulties and ambiguities, or (in the case of the gospels) harmonize a passage to its parallel in another gospel.
- There is disagreement among textual critics as to whether the shorter reading is likely to be original. Some think that longer readings point to elaboration, expansion and clarification by a later scribe. Others, however, make the point that it is easier unconsciously to shorten than to lengthen, and so shorter readings will often betray scribal error. Mark 1.1 may be a case in point (though others have objected that a scribe is unlikely to have slipped into error in the very first line of copying the text!).

In some cases, application of these criteria will point to fairly definite conclusions. The substantial 'longer ending' of Mark (Mark 16.9–20), for example, is regarded as secondary, not only because it is missing in significant early manuscripts such as Sinaiticus and Vaticanus, or that it is replaced by rival endings in some others, but because its style is unlike that of the rest of Mark's Gospel. Furthermore, an original ending at 16.8 can plausibly account for the emergence of this and other endings. A scribe, dissatisfied with such an ending, would have supplied this additional conclusion on the basis of traditions in other gospels.

Similarly, the so-called 'Johannine Comma' in some versions of 1 John 5.7–8 is generally regarded as secondary. It contains a rather explicit Trinitarian reference not found elsewhere in 1 John ('There are three that testify in heaven, the Father, the Word and the Holy Spirit, and these three are one. And there are three that testify on earth . . .'). Moreover, this substantial passage is lacking in all but four late Greek manuscripts. It is hard to see why, if it were original, scribes of such a wide variety of manuscripts would all have omitted it. It may well have begun as a marginal gloss, eventually copied into the text itself.

In certain cases, however, textual critics will be divided over the original reading. For example, what is the original reading of Mark 6.3? In the NRSV this reads: 'Is not this the carpenter, the son of Mary and brother of James and Joses and Judas and Simon, and are not his sisters here with us?' This reading is found in many of our earliest and most significant witnesses, including Sinaiticus, Vaticanus, Alexandrinus and Bezae. However, a number of minuscules have the variant reading 'Is not this the son of the carpenter, [and] of Mary . . .' One way of solving this is to see 'son of the carpenter' as a scribal reverential correction, perhaps harmonizing the text with Matthew 13.55 (cf. Luke. 4.22 'Is not this Joseph's son?'). Growing reverence for Jesus may have caused some to be embarrassed at the suggestion that he had such a lowly occupation. On the other hand, a case could be made for the alternative view: an original 'son of the carpenter' may have been regarded as undermining the doctrine of Christ's virginal conception. 'Son of the carpenter' would be the harder reading, and 'the carpenter' a scribal emendation.

To do

Look at the following passages, and their variant readings (as well as footnotes in your New Testament, you may find it helpful to consult commentaries; if you have Greek, an invaluable resource is Bruce Metzger, 1971, *A Textual Commentary on the Greek New Testament*, Stuttgart: United Bible Societies). Try to work out which is likely to be the original reading, and why the changes might have emerged (for example, due to scribal error or deliberate correction):
• Matthew 27.49
• John 5.3–4
• Romans 1.7
• 1 Corinthians 2.1
• Revelation 13.7

The Problem of Punctuation

Even when the probable original text is established (with a fair degree of certainty), further difficulties arise. These result from the fact that the earliest manuscripts lacked punctuation, as well as spaces between words (see the diagram at the beginning of this chapter). Yet for a text to be intelligible, it needs to be broken up into words, phrases, sentences and paragraphs, together with appropriate punctuation. Where is the sentence break? Does it conclude with a full stop or a question mark? Should certain sections of the text be in inverted commas ('quotation marks')?

One of the major tasks of textual critics (in the case of the Greek text), and of translators (in the case of English and other versions) is to make sense of the letters and words in the text, not least through the provision of sentence divisions and other punctuation. In many cases, this is not problematic or controversial. In other cases, however, decisions about punctuation are crucially important.

One example is in the Prologue to John's Gospel (specifically John 1.3–4). Where should the full stop come in verse 3? At the end, as the verse division suggests? Or at the end of the preceding clause? Different English translations opt for different solutions:

NRSV: 3 All things came into being through him, and without him not one thing came into being. What has come into being 4 in him was life, and the life was the light of all people.

NIV: 3 Through him all things were made; without him nothing was made that has been made. 4 In him was life, and that life was the light of men.

Another example, found in Paul's letter to the Romans, has important implications for Paul's Christology (that is, his belief about Christ). Describing the many gifts God has given to Israel, Paul concludes with this rhetorical flourish (translating literally from the Greek): 'and from whom the Christ according to the flesh the one being over all God blessed into the ages Amen' (Romans 9.5). The key interpretative question is: should there be a full stop only at the end of this verse, or also earlier on? The answer to this question about punctuation is crucial for determining whether in this verse Paul explicitly calls Jesus 'God'. Is 'the one being over all God blessed into the ages' a description of Christ (placing the full stop at the end of the verse)? Or is it a typical Jewish blessing of Israel's God, for bestowing on Israel all the gifts listed in Romans 9.4–5, including the Christ/Messiah (placing the full stop after 'the Christ')? Scholars continue to debate this question, and different answers are reflected in different translations. The New International Version (NIV) goes with the first option:

> Theirs are the patriarchs, and from them is traced the human ancestry of Christ, who is God over all, forever praised! Amen.

The Revised Standard Version (RSV) opts for the second possibility:

> To them belong the patriarchs, and of their race, according to the flesh, is the Christ. God who is over all be blessed for ever. Amen.

The New Revised Standard Version (following the Authorized Version) takes a slightly more ambiguous mediating position:

> To them belong the patriarchs, and from them, according to the flesh, comes the Messiah, who is over all, God blessed forever. Amen.

A third example, also from Paul, affects how we understand his teaching to the Corinthian church regarding a difficult moral case (a man apparently having sexual relations with his stepmother). In 1 Corinthians 5.3–5, to whom is the phrase 'in the name of the Lord Jesus' (verse 4) related? Our answer depends partly on punctuation, and partly on word order. Does it refer to Paul having already pronounced judgement on the man in question 'in the name of the Lord Jesus', thus asserting his apostolic authority? Or is it a reference to the Corinthian liturgical assembly, their coming together 'in the name of the Lord Jesus'? A third possibility, which makes good sense of the Greek word order, is that the phrase is a comment on the man himself, who has 'done this thing in the name of the Lord Jesus'. If so, this is a particularly acute example of the Corinthian misunderstanding of Paul's gospel of freedom in Christ: the man believes that his Christian identity liberates him from any moral constraints. In all three possibilities, punctuation plays a key role.

But punctuating a passage in order to render it intelligible is not simply a case of inserting commas, colons and full stops. Another important issue (especially for the interpretation of 1 Corinthians) is to decide when an author might be quoting from an earlier letter, hymn or liturgical fragment. There are ways in Greek of alerting a reader and audience to the presence of direct speech (the use of the word *hoti*, for example), but this is not always used. In the case of 1 Corinthians, there are good grounds for thinking that at certain points Paul is quoting back to the Corinthians excerpts of a letter they have sent to him. Some English translations of 1 Corinthians 7.1, for example, will mark this out by the use of inverted commas:

> NRSV: 'Now concerning the matters about which you wrote: "It is well for a man not to touch a woman".'

A similar quotation might be found at 8.1: 'Now concerning food sacrificed to idols: we know that "all of us possess knowledge"'. But how far is this to be taken? Some commentators suggest that much of the discussion of prostitutes at 1 Corinthians 6.12–20 should be read as a juxtaposition of Corinthian 'slogans' and Paul's response to them (going further than the suggested interpretation offered by the NRSV).

To do

Look at the following passages where punctuation or word order are an issue (in a range of English translations, or using the Greek New Testament if you are able, and perhaps consulting a commentary or two). In each case, note down the various possible ways of punctuating, and what difference they make. Try to decide which is the most likely punctuation, and why.
- Romans 8.15
- Galatians 2.14–16
- 1 Timothy 3.1
- Revelation 13.8
- Revelation 22.1–2

Which Translation?

Though the task of textual criticism (which some suggest should be seen as an art more than an exact science) is fundamental for New Testament study, in practice most interpreters of the New Testament are content to rely on the conclusions of textual critics rather than engage in the method themselves. This is because most modern readers will read the New Testament not in the original Greek but in a translation into their own language. Although New Testament Greek is still taught in many seminaries and universities, few come to the study of theology with an established background in classical languages.

But herein lies another problem for the would-be New Testament scholar: which translation should I use? A visit to an academic bookseller will reveal a plethora of English translations, editions and formats. Which will be the most useful version for me? Should I buy a New Testament on its own, or one bound together with the Old Testament? Would I be better with a small pocket edition, without distracting notes, or should I purchase a large study edition, with a wealth of introductions, study notes, marginal references and even maps? Should I ensure I have several different versions, so as to have a better sense of the range of possible meanings? Indeed, might certain versions be most appropriate for specific contexts (for example, for reading in church, or studying at my desk, or giving to an enquiring teenager)?

In order to answer these questions, it is certainly important to know the background of and rationale for specific English translations. Some (like the Authorized Version, often known as the King James Version) have taken on a classic status, for their elegance of expression and influence on wider culture. Some are specifically designed for popular dissemination, others for more literary usage. Some are sponsored by particular Christian denominations, often reflecting the interpretative traditions of those denominations and their particular theological stance; others are consciously ecumenical in their production and intended readership.

The different purposes to which the New Testament is put, and the needs of different Christian communities, go some way towards accounting for the variety of English versions. There is, however, one more fundamental reason (which we touched upon in Chapter 2 above): translation is interpretation.

Table 5: Some Current English Translations.

- *Authorized Version* (AV, also known as the King James Version or KJV after King James I who encouraged its production); first published in 1611; a fairly literal translation in elegant English, which has become a classic in its own right
- *Revised Standard Version* (RSV), New Testament first published in 1946; a revision of the AV and its successor, the Revised Version; not so literal, but still keeping close to the original languages; there is an ecumenical edition
- *New Revised Standard Version* (NRSV), published in 1990; a revision of the RSV, taking into account latest manuscript discoveries and advances in textual criticism; has a consistent policy of inclusive language; ecumenical in its appeal and usage
- *Jerusalem Bible* (JB), published in 1966; a Roman Catholic version, essentially a translation of the French Bible de Jérusalem; excellent introductions and study notes; tendency towards paraphrase
- *New Jerusalem Bible* (NJB), published in 1985; a revision of the JB, working from the original languages, and some attempt at inclusive language; notes of the JB updated
- *New English Bible* (NEB), New Testament published in 1961; a British production, instigated by non-conformist churches; offers an elegant, literary translation which nevertheless attempts to avoid 'biblical' language; it opts for 'dynamic transference'
- *Revised English Bible* (REB), published in 1989; a revision of the NEB
- *Good News Bible* (GNB, sometimes called *Today's English Version* or TEV), New Testament published in 1966; deliberately aimed at young or non-churched readership, and therefore using a limited vocabulary, and avoiding words or phrases not in current usage; accessible, but often a paraphrase

continued

- *New International Version* (NIV), New Testament published in 1973; an American Evangelical Protestant translation into contemporary English, aimed at accuracy and 'fidelity to the thought of the biblical writers'; a literary version, designed for both private study and public, liturgical use
- *The Message*, translated by Eugene Peterson (New Testament published in 1994); a translation from the original languages, designed for reading rather than study; a racy, vibrant version of the biblical text, with no verse numbers to interrupt the flow; unashamedly a paraphrase
- *The New Testament*, freshly translated by Nicholas King (published in 2004): a recent translation by an English Jesuit, attempting to convey something of the roughness and freshness of the original, and widely acclaimed by members of a wide variety of churches; described by Archbishop Desmond Tutu as 'like a splash of cold water on one's face'

The word 'translation' comes from the Latin for 'carrying across'. But as those who have studied even elementary French or German at school will know, to carry words and meanings across from one language to another is not a straightforward task. One French word may cover a range of possible English meanings, and vice versa. This is even more the case when dealing with ancient languages, which presuppose very different world-views and cultural perspectives from our own.

In the case of the New Testament, this can create major interpretative problems for translators and commentators alike. In a much debated passage, 1 Corinthians 11.2–16, how should the Greek words *gunē* and *anēr* be translated? These could mean 'woman' or 'wife', and 'man' or 'husband', respectively. Is Paul then dealing with general gender distinctions, or specifically the marital relationship? Or again, at the end of the Lord's Prayer in Matthew (Matthew 6.13), are disciples bidden to be delivered from evil, or rescued from the Evil One (the Devil)? Both are possible interpretations of the Greek phrase.

A second issue for Bible translators is that each language has its own idiomatic phrases which do not necessarily translate easily into another language. The English phrases 'He's no spring chicken!' or 'Don't look a gift horse in the mouth' may well be seriously misunderstood if translated literally word for word. Similar difficulties can emerge when translating the New Testament from Greek into English. Moreover, in some cases matters are further complicated by the fact that underlying the Greek text are idioms reflecting the Semitic languages of Palestine (Hebrew and Aramaic). When John has Jesus say to his mother at the wedding at Cana, 'What to me and to you, woman?' (John 2.4), he is using a Semitic idiom which is odd even in Greek. That literal translation, however, is relatively meaningless in English. Hence the range of alternatives: 'Dear woman, why do you involve me?' (NIV); 'Woman, what concern is that to you and to me?' (NRSV); Woman, how does your concern affect me? (New American Bible); 'Woman, what do you want from me?' (New Jerusalem Bible).

Faced with such difficulties, different panels of translators opt for different translation policies: should one aim as much as possible for 'formal correspondence', that is, using the closest equivalent English words and phrases? Others opt for 'dynamic transference', which attempts to find appropriate English idioms to express the force of the original (as, for example, in the New English Bible). Others might aim for an even more paraphrastic translation, which diverges to a greater or lesser extent from the original words and word order, in order to convey the sense.[16]

A third issue is the extent to which received interpretations, or the theological stance of the translator, leave their mark on the finished translation. In part, this is related to the question of whether the New Testament is the Church's book, to be read and interpreted within the living, worshipping Christian community (though Jewish, agnostic or atheist translators will also bring their presuppositions to the translating task). Whatever one's position on this, it is important to be aware that theological factors may determine how a phrase is translated (and hence some awareness of the background to particular translations is important):

- The Roman Catholic version of the RSV, for example, uses the word 'brethren' whenever the 'brothers of Jesus' are mentioned, reflecting Catholic belief in the perpetual virginity of the Virgin Mary.

- The NRSV is perhaps influenced by later sacramental practice when it translates 1 Timothy 5.22 (literally 'Lay hands on no one quickly') as 'Do not ordain anyone hastily'.
- A particular ethical stance may underlie the older RSV's translation of two somewhat ambiguous Greek words (*malakoi* and *arsenokoitai*) at 1 Corinthians 6.9 by the one English word 'homosexuals' (altered to 'sexual perverts' in later versions, which still fails to convey that two separate groups are at issue).

Finally, the use of Greek puns or double entendres cannot easily be conveyed in an English translation, which may have to opt for one or other possibility. John's Gospel is a particular case in point. When Jesus says to Nicodemus, 'Unless someone is born *anōthen . . .*' (John 3.3), the same Greek word could be translated either 'again' (Nicodemus' misunderstanding) or 'from above' (Jesus' deeper meaning). This double meaning can only be conveyed in an English translation by the use of a footnote. Similarly, when Jesus offers the Samaritan woman *hudōr zōn* (John 4.10), she mistakenly thinks he means 'fresh water' or 'spring water' (hence her rather comical response: 'Sir, you have no bucket . . .!'). In contrast, the reader is meant to understand the alternative meaning of that phrase, 'living water'. Something of that subtlety and verbal ambiguity is sadly lost when the text is translated into English.

To do

Read one of the following passages in two or three different English translations (and refer to the Greek, if you are able). Try to account for the differences in translation. Can you detect any particular translation policies, or theological perspectives? Do the different versions suggest different intended uses?

- Luke 1.1–4
- John 21.1–8
- Romans 8.22–7
- Revelation 21.15–21

Further Reading

Bart D. Ehrman, 1995, 'Textual Criticism of the New Testament', in Joel B. Green (ed.), *Hearing the New Testament: Strategies for Interpretation,* Grand Rapids, Michigan: Eerdmans, pp. 127–45.

Keith Elliott and Ian Moir, 1995, *Manuscripts and the Text of the Greek New Testament,* Edinburgh: T. & T. Clark.

Bruce Metzger, 1971, *A Textual Commentary on the Greek New Testament,* Stuttgart: United Bible Societies.

Henry Wansbrough, 2006, *The Story of the Bible: How it Came to Us,* London: Darton, Longman and Todd.

5

Why Four Gospels?

Four or More or Less?

Once one has decided upon a basic Greek text, or selected a particular New Testament translation and edition, a new question may well emerge: why does this collection begin with *four* gospels, giving four rather different accounts of the life and ministry of Jesus? Isn't this a problem for Christianity? Why not a single authoritative gospel, to rule out any discrepancy or ambiguity? Or why not more than one? Doesn't this restriction in number amount to a silencing of rival voices (such as the *Gospel of Thomas*, or the *Gospel of Mary Magdalene*)?

Some of these are not new questions. Rather, they have been asked almost from the beginning. A survey of the first 200 or 300 years of Christian history reveals five basic answers to this question:

• *Choose one gospel out of these four:* this is essentially the solution of the second-century figure Marcion. Arguably, Marcion's problem was his inability to read the Bible, especially the Old Testament, in a non-literal way. Reading literally, he concluded that the God of the Old Testament could not be equated with the God and Father of Jesus, but was a lesser creator god. Hence he rejected not only the Old Testament but also what he considered to be 'judaized' New Testament writings. His truncated canon contained ten letters of Paul (it lacked the Pastoral Epistles), and a filleted version of the gospel attributed to Paul's companion Luke.

- *Allow a multiplicity of gospels:* giving a much wider range of 'Jesuses', or perspectives on Jesus, some of them quite esoteric. Diverse Gnostic groups produced a vast body of literature, including a significant number of books given the title 'gospels' (though not all of them are narratives). Many of these were rediscovered near Nag Hammadi in Upper Egypt in 1945; an accessible English translation is edited by James M. Robinson, *The Nag Hammadi Library in English* (2nd edition, Leiden: Brill, 1988). Other non-canonical gospels have also survived from the early centuries, including infancy gospels which tell us much about growing Christian piety and tradition. A relatively cheap and accessible, if incomplete, collection is *The Other Gospels,* edited by Ron Cameron (Cambridge: Lutterworth Press, 1982).
- *Prefer the oral tradition to written texts:* this is what the second-century Bishop Papias called 'the living and abiding voice'. The spoken testimony to Jesus, passed on by recognized authority figures, was somehow more reliable or authoritative than anything written. This is a reminder of the essentially oral culture within which Christianity emerged and developed. One of the most interesting questions, indeed, is why gospel narratives came to be *written* at all.[17] It was not a foregone conclusion that the followers of Jesus should produce written texts.
- *Combine the accounts of Matthew, Mark, Luke and John into a harmonized version:* most famously, this was the approach of Tatian, who c.172 CE produced the so-called *Diatessaron* (literally 'through four'). This conflation and harmonization served as the definitive text in the Syrian church for a couple of centuries. It had the advantage of providing a single voice rather than the sometimes discordant voices of different accounts.
- *Regard these four, not harmonized but side by side, as authoritative:* our four-gospel canon. This is the position the Church opted for, famously defended by the second-century father Irenaeus of Lyons. Indeed, a number of scholars have taken up the suggestion of T. C. Skeat that it was the desire to have all four gospels bound together which led to the early adoption of the codex by Christians.[18] One written gospel, or no written gospel, or a harmonized gospel, is not sufficient to convey the truth about Christ; on the other hand, there needs to be discernment to adjudicate between the multiplicity of written gospels emerging.

Irenaeus is not the originator of the fourfold gospel; codices containing the four canonical gospels seem to have been in existence before he wrote. However, his defence of the four-gospel canon is memorable:

> It is not possible that the Gospels can be either more or fewer in number than they are. For, since there are four zones of the world in which we live, and four principal winds, while the Church is scattered throughout all the world, and the 'pillar and ground' of the Church is the Gospel and the spirit of life; it is fitting that she should have four pillars, breathing out immortality on every side, and vivifying men afresh. From which fact, it is evident that the Word, the Artificer of all, He that sitteth upon the cherubim, and contains all things, He who was manifested to men, has given us the Gospel under four aspects, but bound together by one Spirit. (Irenaeus, *Against Heresies* 3.11.8)[19]

Some of his arguments sound decidedly odd (not to say unscientific!) to the modern ear. However, in Irenaeus' world where pattern and order were so important – built into the very structure of the universe – his defence would have been compelling. A gospel intended for the whole world, and for all cultures, must have been revealed in a manner that reflects the fourfold nature of that world, manifesting diversity in unity. In Irenaeus' words, it is given 'under four aspects' or as a 'fourfold Gospel' (Greek *tetramorphon to euangelion*; Latin *quadriforme Evangelium*).

> **Reflection**
>
> What are the pros and cons of each of the five early Christian alternatives?

What is a Gospel?

But why are these four books called 'gospels'? The English word 'gospel' is derived from the Old English *gōdspel* meaning 'good news' or 'good tidings'.

It translates the Greek *euangelion*, which is used throughout the New Testament to describe the good news of God's kingdom proclaimed by Jesus, or the good news of what God has done in Jesus. It is used in this sense by Paul (for example, Romans 1.3; 1 Corinthians 1.17), and indeed by what many think to be the earliest of the written 'gospels', Mark (Mark 1.1 'The beginning of the good news of Jesus Christ, the Son of God'). In other words, the original gospel is essentially oral. It is good news preached or proclaimed, the 'good announcement'.

Moreover, the term is not a purely Christian innovation. Greek-speaking Jews, and Christians from a Jewish background, might detect echoes of the prophet Isaiah, who proclaimed: 'How beautiful upon the mountains are the feet of the messenger who announces peace, who brings good news, who announces salvation, who says to Zion, "Your God reigns"' (Isaiah 52.7). Jesus' proclamation that God's reign is breaking in through his ministry would have evoked just such Isaian prophecies (though the LXX of Isaiah uses the verb 'to proclaim good news' rather than the noun). Those from a pagan background might contrast this 'gospel' with the rival 'gospels' (*euangelia*) associated with the emperor as 'Saviour' and bringer of peace. Set against this political background, the Christian message would have been subversive indeed![20]

Whatever the background, there is ultimately only one Christian gospel. There may be different human communicators of it, presenting it in different language. But the gospel itself is one. On this, Paul is particularly insistent: 'But even if we or an angel from heaven should proclaim to you a gospel contrary to what we proclaimed to you, let that one be accursed!' (Galatians 1.8).

By the early second century, however, there is some evidence that the narrative books of, for example, Matthew and Luke were being referred to as 'gospels' in the plural. In other words, we have moved from 'the gospel' as a primarily oral message to 'a gospel' as something written. Nevertheless, this does not override the original understanding. In Irenaeus' words, Matthew, Mark, Luke and John present the one gospel fourfold or 'under four aspects'. Strictly speaking, these four books are called 'the Gospel according to Matthew', 'according to Mark', etc. (titles attached to the four books at least since the second century, and found in most contemporary versions).

But what kind of books are they? Here scholarship seems to have shifted ground considerably in recent years. For much of the twentieth century, scholars saw the canonical gospels as *sui generis*, that is, unlike any other type of book in ancient literature. They were certainly not biographies of Jesus. Rather, they were closer to the folklorish literature typical of primarily oral societies, made up of stories which were reshaped in the retelling, according to the needs of different audiences. Or they were documents of faith, less interested in the 'Jesus of history' than in the 'Christ of faith'. As the twentieth century progressed, more emphasis came to be placed on the creative role of the evangelists themselves in shaping their material in order to proclaim the truth about Jesus as they understood it (see the section on redaction criticism in Chapter 6).

Clearly as 'gospel' or 'good news', the canonical gospels *are* documents of faith. But this does not rule out their use of, and similarities to, literary antecedents. The early twentieth-century denial of the 'biographical' nature of the gospels was in no small part due to the exaggerated claims of nineteenth-century scholars, who did not always note the differences between biographies of the ancient world and the increasingly popular modern biography, with its emphasis upon the subject's background, formative influences and psychological development. Following the lead of recent scholars such as Charles Talbert and especially Richard Burridge,[21] a more nuanced answer is generally given to the question: 'What are the gospels?' Burridge especially has shown the similarities between ancient Graeco-Roman biographies and our Matthew, Mark, Luke and John. In short, the gospels are once again regarded as 'lives of Jesus': not in the sense of modern biographies, but in the sense of ancient 'lives' (Greek *bioi*).

To do

With the help of a concordance, select some passages (there are quite a lot!) in which the phrase 'gospel' or 'good news' (Greek *euangelion*) occurs. Does it always refer to the same thing? Does any author use it in a different way to others? Are there any passages in which the term might be used to refer to a gospel book?

Four Portraits

The differences between the four gospels are often explained using the analogy of paintings or portraits. A visit to London's National Gallery provides a good illustration. Here one finds a large number of portraits of Jesus of Nazareth. Let us consider just four, painted within a century of each other.

Jacopo Tintoretto's *Christ Washing his Disciples' Feet* (*c*.1556) portrays Christ in servant mode (though his bright halo betrays his divine luminosity), kneeling at the feet of the protesting Peter. In Velázquez's *Kitchen Scene with Christ in the House of Martha and Mary* (1618), Jesus is seated solidly as teacher, his left hand raised as if illustrating a point, while his would-be female disciples listen intently. *Christ Blessing the Children* by Nicholaes Maes (1652–3), a pupil of Rembrandt, reveals a compassionate Christ, laying his hand tenderly on the head of a little girl. There is a hint of sadness in his eyes, as if he sees what the future holds. Finally, an enraged Jesus wields a whip at the drivers of oxen and sheep in Jacopo Bassano's *The Purification of the Temple* (probably painted about 1580). Each of these very different paintings conveys one particular aspect of the gospel portrayal of Jesus, viewed through the lens of the artist's perception and cultural heritage (they can be viewed online at the National Gallery's website: www.nationalgallery.org.uk/collection).

Is Christ to be best viewed as an angry person, protesting at religious abuses as did the Old Testament prophets? Or is he the compassionate Lord, who reaches out to children, the sick, and those in other kind of need? Is he most appropriately understood as a teacher, or as a self-emptying servant figure? Or are all these different and necessary aspects of the one Jesus? This question is sharply posed by the gospels themselves. In Matthew, Jesus wears the prayer-shawl of the pious Jew, who teaches Israel in a manner that evokes the authority of Israel's great teacher Moses. Mark's bewildering Jesus often pushes the boundaries of what pious Jews might think acceptable, even to the extent of undermining Jewish kosher laws. Luke presents a Jesus who, although brought up in accordance with the law of Moses, is easily a match for the greatest heroes of the Graeco-Roman world. Finally, in John, we are left wondering whether Jesus belongs here at all, or whether he is a visitor from another world.

Irenaeus already detects this diversity in his likening of the four gospels to the four cherubim witnessed by Ezekiel and John of Patmos (bearing the characteristics of a lion, a calf or ox, a human being and an eagle: Ezekiel 1; Revelation 4). For Irenaeus, John is full of lion-like confidence, expressing Jesus' royal power. Luke emphasizes Christ's priestly character, the calf being a sacrificial animal. The human Matthew describes Christ's human descent from David and Abraham. Finally, Mark begins with the eagle-like Spirit of prophecy, speaking through Isaiah, and about to descend upon Jesus at the Jordan (*Against Heresies* 3.11.8). In later Christian usage, following Jerome, Mark and John are reversed. In the standard symbols found in mosaics, paintings and illustrated gospel manuscripts, Mark = the lion, Luke = the ox, Matthew = the human figure, John = the eagle.

Recent New Testament scholarship, as we shall see in the next two chapters, has re-emphasized Irenaeus' recognition that the gospel writers speak of the same Christ differently. Redaction criticism of the gospels has increasingly stressed the role of the individual evangelists in shaping their material in line with their own particular theological understanding, cultural context and sense of purpose. Mark's portrait is not the same as Matthew's – even if the two overlap significantly in their contents – and should be allowed to speak for itself. More recent narrative approaches have tended to view the gospels as four distinct stories, which need to be read in their entirety in order for their impact to be felt. Either way, the fourfold nature of the canonical gospels is regarded as a benefit rather than a misfortune.

To do

Look at the four gospel accounts of Jesus' death (Matthew 27.45–54; Mark 15.33–9; Luke 23.44–8; John 19.28–30; this is best done with the help of a synopsis). Pay particular attention to the portrayal of Jesus, and his dying words. What does each suggest to you about the respective evangelist's understanding of Jesus?

Intended Audiences

One of the ways in which New Testament scholars have accounted for this 'fourfold' nature of the written gospels is by appeal to intended audiences. Human authors generally write with a particular audience in mind, even if they cannot be sure who will read their work in practice. What they recount, and how they recount it, will normally be shaped with such an audience in view. Unless a text is going to remain largely unintelligible, an author will want to explain terms or customs with which that audience is unlikely to be familiar. So, for example, many of the early Church fathers believed that Matthew had written his Gospel with Jewish audiences in mind, while Luke was the gospel for the Gentile world.

But how should we envisage the gospel audiences? In recent decades, scholars have often envisaged the gospels as written for the evangelists' own communities, that is, the local Christian church of which they were a part. A classic work along these lines is Raymond Brown's *Community of the Beloved Disciple*, subtitled 'The Life, Loves, and Hates of an Individual Church in New Testament Times'. For Brown, in other words (building on the earlier work of J. Louis Martyn) the Fourth Gospel is written on two levels.[22] The level of the narrative is the historical ministry of Jesus of Nazareth; the deeper level, which has left its mark on the narrative, is the ongoing story of the risen Jesus active in the life and experience of the recipients of this gospel (the so-called 'Johannine community'). Clues have been left in the text which tell us about the past and current experience of this community, with its very distinctive way of speaking about Jesus, its ethnic make-up (including Jews, Samaritans and Gentiles), its somewhat stormy relationship with other Christian communities, and its bitter experience of expulsion from the synagogue and subsequent persecution. Others similarly interpret the remaining gospels in terms of 'the Matthean community', 'the Marcan community' and 'the Lucan community'.

Recently, this view that gospels were written essentially for internal consumption, with specific communities in mind, has been seriously challenged. An important book here is the 1998 collection edited by Richard Bauckham. Its title, *The Gospels for All Christians*, reveals its alternative thesis.[23]

According to its contributors, the gospels were intended for a wide general Christian readership from the start. The 'community' hypothesis, they contend, is more appropriate to letters of Paul (explicitly written to address particular problems within specific Christian churches) than to narrative works like the gospels. It is particularly inappropriate for the gospels, as Richard Burridge comments in his contribution to Bauckham's volume, if they belong to the ancient genre of *bios*. It replaces a literal reading of the text with an 'allegorical' reading which has failed to produce a scholarly consensus. Moreover, it fuses, and therefore confuses, an author's *background* with his or her *audience*.

Bauckham and his colleagues have sparked an important debate which remains live in New Testament scholarship. Counter-challenges have been made to their call for a paradigm shift.[24] Many of Bauckham's examples about Christian networks and ease of communication come from the second rather than first century, for example. Nor are we without precedents for religious groups producing texts – and not simply letters – for internal consumption (the Jewish Qumran scrolls are a classic example). Indeed, the Johannine Epistles within the New Testament itself reveal that there were groups of 'Johannine Christians' who regarded themselves as distinct from other Christians, even if they were not located in one place, or in total isolation. A number of scholars have argued for a mediating position which avoids extreme claims on either side of the debate.

What most if not all of those involved in the debate agree upon, however, is that the evangelists' *background,* including the community or communities of which they were part, has impacted on what and how they wrote (whether or not those communities were also intended audiences). If Matthew was writing in Syrian Antioch in the 80s (one common hypothesis), for example, that bilingual, urban, cosmopolitan environment will have affected the way in which he describes the rural, Galilean ministry of Jesus some 50 or so years earlier. Location, culture and cultural assumptions, ethnic make-up of the background community, language of writing (Greek rather than Hebrew or Aramaic) are all likely to have contributed to the shape and content of our written gospels.

The Synoptic Problem

Our discussion of particular passages has already drawn attention to the often close similarity in content, wording and order between the first three canonical gospels. Approximately 90 per cent of the contents of Mark's Gospel are paralleled in Matthew, while another 50 per cent are found in Luke. These similarities are sufficient to convince the majority of scholars that there is a literary relationship between these three. That is, one (or more) of these gospels served as a written source for its successor (or successors). Indeed, this much is implied by the prologue to Luke's Gospel:

> Since *many have undertaken to set down an orderly account* of the events that have been fulfilled among us, just as they were handed on to us by those who from the beginning were eyewitnesses and servants of the word, *I too decided*, after investigating everything carefully from the very first, *to write an orderly account* for you, most excellent Theophilus, so that you may know the truth concerning the things about which you have been instructed. (Luke 1.1–4; italics mine)

The question this poses – how are Matthew, Mark and Luke related to one another? – is called by scholars the *Synoptic Problem*. Solving the Synoptic Problem has been regarded as important for at least two reasons: First, if we can isolate an evangelist's sources (for example, determine that Mark was a source for Matthew, or Matthew for Luke), it is easier to see how he has altered those sources, and thus what he is trying to say. Second, it has often been thought that isolating earlier sources will bring us closer to the 'historical Jesus'. This second point is debatable: an arguably later text like John may well preserve traditions about Jesus more primitive that those found in earlier gospels. Nevertheless, some solution to the Synoptic Problem is a practical requirement for engagement with the 'Jesus quest'.

Some basic data has been noted by careful study of the first three gospels in parallel, which needs to be taken into account in any solution to the problem (this data is well expressed by E. P. Sanders and Margaret Davies in their 1989 *Studying the Synoptic Gospels*, London/Philadelphia: SCM/Trinity Press International, ch. 3, upon which the following draws):

- In the *triple tradition* (that is, when all three synoptic gospels have a passage in common), all three often follow the same sequence. When either Matthew or Luke departs from that sequence, the other generally follows Mark's sequence (this is known as 'the argument from order').
- In the triple tradition, there are often substantial agreements in wording between Matthew and Mark against Luke, and between Luke and Mark against Matthew (when either Matthew or Luke disagrees with Mark, the other generally agrees).
- In the triple tradition, agreement between Matthew and Luke generally begins where there is a Marcan parallel and ends where the Marcan parallel ends. On a macro-level, for example, Matthew and Luke's infancy narratives and resurrection appearance stories diverge considerably, where there is no Marcan parallel; they are close in the narrative about John the Baptist (where Mark begins), and in the narrative of the empty tomb (where Mark ends). This phenomenon also occurs in individual stories.
- Nevertheless, there are a very large number of points in the triple tradition where Matthew and Luke agree against Mark, omitting or adding the same word or phrase, including substantial phrases such as 'Who is it that struck you?' (Matthew 26.68 // Luke 22.64b). These are known as the 'minor agreements'.
- There is also in Matthew and Luke a large body of shared material not found in Mark (Sanders and Davies estimate 200 verses or so): this is called the *double tradition*. At times there is virtually verbatim agreement between the two gospels; at other times they diverge considerably in wording (as in the Beatitudes).
- The order of this double tradition often differs significantly (though not always!) in the two gospels.

Various solutions have been offered to this problem. An early position, following St Augustine (hence the *Augustinian Hypothesis*), follows the normal canonical order: Matthew wrote first, followed by Mark, while Luke used both his predecessors.

The most widespread solution in contemporary New Testament scholarship, however, places Mark before Matthew. Known as the *Two Source Theory*, it claims that Mark is the earliest of the three synoptics, and was used by both Matthew and Luke as one of their two main sources (accounting for the triple tradition). As their second source, they independently used another source, now lost, containing mainly sayings of Jesus. This is known by scholars as Q (from the German word for 'source', *Quelle*). First proposed in Germany in the nineteenth century, it was popularized in twentieth-century British scholarship by B. H. Streeter. There are several variations on this, including the *Four Source Theory*, to account for material in both Matthew (M = Matthew's special material) and Luke (L = Luke's special material) that is neither triple nor double tradition.

The existence of Q remains a hypothesis which has not convinced everyone, however. One rival theory to the Two Source Theory dispenses with Q by reviving the ancient view of Matthean Priority. This is the so-called *Griesbach Hypothesis* (confusingly, also called the *Two Gospel Hypothesis*), after J. J. Griesbach who proposed it at the end of the eighteenth century. More recently it has been revived by William Farmer and is particularly popular in North America. According to this theory, Matthew was the first gospel, used by Luke; Mark then combined both gospels in his work (hence 'Two Gospel Hypothesis').

There is an alternative theory to the Two Source Hypothesis, growing in popularity, which retains what many see as the strengths of Marcan priority while dispensing with Q. Associated with Austin Farrer (so sometimes called the *Farrer Theory*, though also *Mark without Q*), Michael Goulder and, more recently, Mark Goodacre, it proposes that Mark wrote first, was expanded by Matthew, and that Luke used both Mark and Matthew in the composition of his Gospel.

Two further issues are also on the agenda of synoptic study. The first relates to the question of orality raised, for example, by James Dunn (and mentioned in Chapter 3 above). The standard theories often treat the tradition as essentially literary and fixed (such that one can place great significance in individual word changes). But what if some of the differences between the gospels are due to oral tradition as opposed to written sources? Some

Figure 1: Major Solutions to the Synoptic Problem.

Augustinian Hypothesis

Two Source Hypothesis

Four Source Hypothesis

Griesbach Hypothesis (Two Gospel Hypothesis)

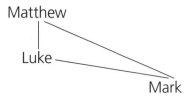

Farrer Theory (Marcan priority without Q)

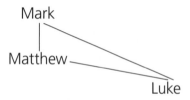

more complex solutions have attempted to factor this into the equation (see Sanders and Davies, *Studying the Synoptic Gospels*, ch. 6).

The second issue is whether John should be included in the equation. Obviously, the relationship between John and the synoptics is of a different order to that between Matthew, Mark and Luke. There are relatively few direct parallels, and a number of scholars believe that those can be accounted for on the basis of common oral traditions rather than literary dependence of John on any synoptic gospel. The jury, it must be admitted, is out on this question. Nevertheless, that does not mean that John should be sidelined, especially when it comes to discussion of 'historical Jesus' questions. The Fourth Gospel may well preserve primitive and valuable traditions about Jesus independently of the other three. Indeed, some gospel synopses (for example, that of Kurt Aland) have columns for all four gospels. In addition, Barbara Shellard has recently revived the theory suggested by F. Lamar Cribbs, that Luke rather than John was the fourth gospel to be written, and that he used all three of his predecessors as sources.[25] This adds a whole new slant to the question of the relationship between John and at least one of the synoptics, though not in the order generally perceived.

Reading Synoptically

The remainder of this chapter will be taken up with a specific worked example of synoptic reading: the appearance of John the Baptist (Matthew 3.1–6 // Mark 1.2–6 // Luke 3.1–6 // John 1.19–23). It is an interesting passage, and one of the rare occasions where there is a Johannine parallel. For those using a synopsis, the passage can be found at Aland §13, or Throckmorton §1.

Synoptic Relationships

A first look suggests considerable divergence between the accounts (and John, as so often, is very different). Nevertheless, a closer look will reveal some verbatim agreement between the three synoptic accounts, suggesting a literary relationship. As so often in the triple tradition, Mark seems to be the middle term linking Matthew and Luke (explicable by Marcan priority, though not requiring it). Try to work out where this is the case. Note also those points at which Matthew and Luke agree against Mark. What might this suggest about synoptic relationships?

Mark's account

Looking at Mark's account first, the following points are worth noting:
- This is the beginning of Mark's Gospel (after the title at Mark 1.1): it contains an Old Testament quotation (attributed to Isaiah, though in fact it combines texts from Exodus, Malachi and Isaiah), and the appearance of John in the wilderness.
- Two features explain to us who John is in Mark's eyes (inherited from earlier tradition): the prophetic citations in verses 2–3 (Elijah returned, and the voice preparing the way of the Lord), and the statement about John's clothing in verse 6 (cf. the description of Elijah at 2 Kings 1.8 – 'A hairy man, with a leather belt around his waist').
- John's role as forerunner is to call people to repentance (notice the poetic licence in verse 5 about those who 'were going out' to him!), and preaches a 'baptism of repentance'.

Matthew's account

In many ways, Matthew is very similar to Mark. This makes the differences all the more striking:
- Matthew has already had two chapters of infancy narratives, in which he has told us who Jesus is and where he comes from (is Matthew 'filling in the gap' in Mark's more mysterious account?)
- Marcan priority makes good sense of Matthew's account here: he corrects Mark's misquotation by omitting at this point the Malachi quotation (as does Luke: they both have it, in exactly the same Greek form, later in their gospels (Matthew 11.10 // Luke 7.27)), and delays the Isaiah quotation (as does Luke) until he has introduced John the Baptist.

- He also clarifies the geographical location in verse 1: John is active in the wilderness 'of Judea'.
- He seems to feel embarrassment that Jesus submitted to a 'baptism of repentance for the forgiveness of sins'; hence his reworking of the Baptist's words in verse 2, which also links more closely what John does to what Jesus does (perhaps stressing that Jesus, not John, sets the agenda).
- Throughout his Gospel, as in verse 2, he uses 'kingdom of heaven' rather than 'kingdom of God'
- He agrees with Mark in seeing John as Elijah returned: in fact, he makes this even more explicit by telling us the details of John's clothing before he tells of those who came for John's baptism (compare also Matthew 17.9–13 with Mark 9.9–13).

Luke's account

- Like Matthew, Luke also has two chapters of infancy narratives: his tell us not only who Jesus is, but also who John the Baptist is (the prophet to prepare the way of the Lord, 'with the spirit and power of Elijah').
- But though John may come in the spirit of Elijah, Luke seems to draw back from identifying the two: he omits reference to John's clothing (he also omits the discussion after the Transfiguration found in Mark and Matthew); indeed, as his Gospel progresses, it will become clear that he sees Jesus as the great prophet in the mould of Elijah and Elisha, as well as Moses.
- Instead, Luke's major insertion at the beginning (verses 1–2) highlights one of his key concerns: setting the gospel in the context of the broader history of the empire as well as Palestine.
- He also extends the citation from Isaiah (verses 4–6), so that it concludes with the phrase 'and all flesh shall see the salvation of God' (again expressing his universal concern); 'salvation' and the related word 'Saviour' are important for Luke's understanding of the good news, intelligible to the wider Graeco-Roman world.

John's account

- The Johannine parallel is wholly different, with little verbatim agreement; however, it agrees with the other three in connecting the passage from Isaiah 40.3 to John the Baptist.
- If it describes the same event (the people coming out to John), John views it as a dialogue between the Baptist and priests and Levites from Jerusalem (note the negative portrayal of 'the Jews' throughout the Fourth Gospel).
- John's dialogue seems to run clear contrary to what is claimed in Matthew and Mark (but downplayed somewhat in Luke), namely, that John is to be identified with Elijah. This is denied here with a resounding 'I am not' (verse 21).
- For the Fourth Gospel, John is not 'the Baptist' but simply 'the voice'. Indeed, there is no indication whatever that John is baptizing at this stage (this is stated later on, in John 3, but played down here). Nowhere does the evangelist claim that John baptized Jesus (why might the evangelist want to downplay this?).

To do

Select two further passages from a synopsis, and study them as for the above passage. What is the overlap between them, and what does this suggest about their literary relationship? How does each account differ, and how might one account for that? Is any evangelist correcting another, or interpreting the same material in a different way?

Further Reading

Richard Burridge, 2004, *What are the Gospels? A Comparison with Graeco-Roman Biography*, 2nd edition; Grand Rapids, Michigan/Cambridge: Eerdmans.

Richard A. Burridge, 1994, *Four Gospels, One Jesus? A Symbolic Reading*, London: SPCK.

Mark Goodacre, 2001, *The Synoptic Problem: A Way through the Maze,* London and New York: Sheffield Academic Press.

Rudolf Schnackenburg, 1995, *Jesus in the Gospels: A Biblical Christology,* ET Louisville, Kentucky: Westminster John Knox Press.

Graham Stanton, 2002, *The Gospels and Jesus,* 2nd edition; Oxford: Oxford University Press.

6

Reading Historically

Exegetical Archaeology

Visitors to the ruined Galilean town of Capernaum – the place Jesus made the centre of his public ministry – will be confronted with a rather striking twentieth-century building. Looking somewhat like a concrete spaceship, it straddles the ancient ruins beneath, enabling them to be inspected by the pilgrims and tourists. This is the Church of St Peter, built over what many believe to be the site of Simon Peter's house, where Jesus healed Peter's mother-in-law (Mark 1.29–31). But that first-century house is not immediately in evidence. The first thing a visitor sees is this modern church. Below that, however, archaeologists have excavated the remains of an octagonal church of the fifth century. This church was constructed over a fourth-century complex, itself built out of a set of domestic dwellings, one of which seems to have been restructured for public use at some point in the mid-first century. In other words, subsequent generations have built upon the site of Peter's house, such that the earliest level is now covered by several later layers. Considerable imagination is required for a pilgrim wishing to visualize the humble first-century house of Simon the fisherman.

This is a phenomenon with which archaeologists are only too familiar. Given that subsequent generations build upon the foundations of their predecessors and that consequently street levels rise over time, the deeper one digs the further back in time one goes. Recent construction work for a new shopping centre in the city of Canterbury, for example, uncovered significant remains from its Roman and medieval past. Back in the Holy Land, the tell (mound) of ancient Jericho, excavated by the famous British archaeologist Kathleen Kenyon, enables us to see the various stages of this city's occupation laid upon each other.

In a similar way, historical reading of the New Testament, especially the gospels, has often been described by the archaeological metaphor. Like an archaeological site, layers of reflection and interpretation have been built upon earlier tradition, adapting it to new purposes, such that one needs to 'dig' beneath the surface of the text in order to uncover earlier stages in the tradition. Taking the gospels as the paradigm, the gospel text is like the grass on the surface. Scratch the topsoil a little, and clues may be found as to the time, context and interests of the evangelist. Dig down to the next level, and you will find clues as to the tradition prior to its incorporation into the gospel (sources used, development of the oral tradition and the uses to which it was put, etc.). The level below that is the level of Jesus and his pre-Easter ministry. Many 'exegetical archaeologists' will stop digging at this point. However, a good case can be made for continuing the dig, for not even Jesus emerges in a vacuum. Rather, he emerges out of the Jewish tradition (and most especially the Old Testament), and needs to be understood upon that foundation. The next level down, then, would be the tradition of Israel.

So, reading Matthew's Gospel will not give us immediate access to how Christians prior to Matthew understood the healing of the centurion's servant (Matthew 8.5–13), or Jesus' overturning the tables of the money-changers (Matthew 21.12–13). If one wants to know whether Jesus is likely to have been called 'Son of God' prior to his resurrection (for example, Matthew 14.33), or the original version of the parable of the sower (Matthew 13.3–9), one needs to 'dig' even deeper beneath the text (looking at parallel passages in the other gospels also).

While this archaeological approach to exegesis has been most obviously applied to the gospels, it can be used of other New Testament writings, including the letters of Paul. When Paul cites from the tradition about Jesus' last supper (1 Corinthians 11.23–5), he is drawing upon a historical level prior to that of the composition of his Corinthian letter. The prologue to Luke's Gospel suggests that, even in Acts, earlier sources and oral traditions about the early community in Jerusalem, or Paul's various visits to Ephesus, have been incorporated into the final text. Some scholars even think that the visionary book of Revelation reuses existing traditions (for example, Revelation 11.1–2; 22.20), and therefore provides a glimpse of levels of Christian life and thought prior to John.

Various methods have been developed to ask these historical questions about the New Testament: source criticism; form criticism; redaction criticism (and the related method called composition criticism). These will be explored in more detail later in the chapter. See Figure 2 for a visual description of this archaeological metaphor.

Of course, like any metaphor, this archaeological one has its limitations. In Chapter 3, we noted James Dunn's claim that many scholars have not taken the essentially oral nature of early Christian tradition seriously enough. With oral tradition, there is not only one 'original' version of a story or saying which is then elaborated upon (some would say 'corrupted') by later interpreters. Rather, there may have been several versions of the same tradition from the start. This means that we cannot always assume that there is a 'pure' version which can be recovered by 'stripping away' later accretions (or by digging down through the layers). This is an important point. Nevertheless, this does not render the 'archaeological' approach illegitimate. The gospels themselves provide concrete evidence that – at least at a literary level – the New Testament authors reshaped traditional material, adding new layers of meaning to it. Used judiciously, this 'archaeological' reading remains a useful one for addressing historical questions.

The Importance of History

Why is history important when it comes to the New Testament writings? There are a number of possible reasons. First, historical study of the New Testament acknowledges that these texts have a history. They arise at a particular time and in a particular place, and are affected by particular issues and interests. Questions about that setting, the author who wrote at that time, and the author's intended audience or readership, are significant for interpretation. As we saw in Chapter 2, there is debate as to how far the author's intention in writing (if recoverable) is determinative for the text's meaning. Nevertheless, many interpreters continue to argue strongly that

Figure 2: Exegetical Archaeology.

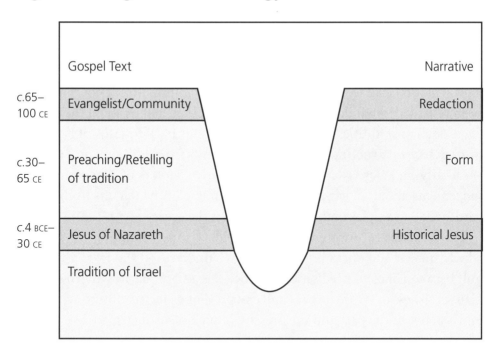

the author's setting is at least one important ingredient in understanding what these books mean. Attention to Philippi in the first century, as well as our sources for Paul's visits to that city, will aid our understanding of his letter to the Philippians. Some knowledge of the particular challenges for urban Christians in the late first century may illuminate passages in the Acts of the Apostles (even if we cannot locate precisely its place of writing).

This quest for the author, and the author's context, is occasionally made more difficult (but perhaps even more interesting!) by the likelihood that some texts have more than one author, at least in their final form. The Fourth Gospel, for example, not only claims the authority of 'the disciple whom Jesus loved'; the final chapter concludes with others (described as 'we' and 'I') attesting to the valid witness of this original disciple (John 21.24–5). Should we then attend only to the authors/editors of the final form of this gospel? Or should the original disciple (or the original evangelist, if the two are different) be the main focus of our history enquiry? Or are both significant in the historical interpretation of John?

Second, as the archaeological paradigm reveals, the New Testament writings have a prehistory. They draw upon existing traditions about Jesus and early Christian creeds, prayers and hymns, and often reuse and reshape earlier written sources. Some of the historical questions asked about the texts are precisely focused on this pre-history (the 'lower levels' in our archaeological model): can we isolate the sources and traditions used? how have they been reshaped? what do these underlying traditions tell us about the earliest Christian communities? how far do they take us back to Jesus of Nazareth himself? Reconstructing early Christian hymns from Philippians 2 or John 1, identifying a 'Jerusalem' source in the early chapters of Acts, or making judgements about an earlier form of the parable of the tenants in the vineyard, are all examples of this kind of historical enquiry.

Third, historical awareness helps avoid misunderstanding the way in which ancient audiences are likely to have understood the text. There is a gulf between ancient Mediterranean societies and modern Western society. Consciousness of this historical gulf can prevent us too readily drawing analogies between the past and the present. Some knowledge of ancient understandings of marriage, for example, are important for interpreting Paul's comments on the subject in 1 Corinthians 7. An awareness of the ancient Jewish concern that priests and Levites should avoid contact with corpses, so as not to be barred from performing their duties in the Temple, will illuminate the famous parable of the Good Samaritan. The shock value for Luke's readers would be that Jesus sides not with those who do their religious duty – the priest and the Levite – but with the despised Samaritan. The discovery that in the first century the goddess Roma (the personification of the city of Rome) was sometimes portrayed as reclining on the city's seven hills makes it likely that the first audiences of Revelation would have identified her with the prostitute Babylon that John sees seated on a seven-headed monster (Revelation 17).

Fourth, orthodox Christianity has always claimed to be a religion rooted in history. For Christians, God became human in Jesus Christ. The Word of God is revealed in and through the written words of human authors. Hence, historical enquiry into the Christian movement, its writings, and its founding figure Jesus, is an inevitable consequence of this truth claim. Scholars debate fiercely about the significance of 'the historical Jesus', and how one should go about asking historical questions of Jesus (see Chapter 2 in the companion volume to this, *SCM Studyguide to the Books of the New Testament*). But most would accept that such historical enquiry is not only legitimate but also illuminating.

Thinking historically is, however, as much an art as it is a science. Obviously, there is a certain amount that can be learnt. Knowledge of the Jewish and classical sources, for example, will give a more rounded picture of the world within which these writings were produced. Study of maps in a study Bible or Bible atlas is indispensable for locating the events being described (for example, the relative locations of Capernaum, the Decapolis, Samaria and Jerusalem), as well as the later geographical settings of the authors (for example, Rome, Ephesus, Antioch). Useful bible atlases are listed in the introduction to this studyguide. However, some of the finest examples of historical reconstruction (and historians always work with hypothetical reconstructions, which they test against the evidence) are aided by the human imagination.

We have already mentioned Gerd Theissen's novel, which reconstructs the contexts within which Galilean disciples would have shared and honed their stories about Jesus. Paula Fredriksen's excellent study of Jesus contains an imaginative reconstruction of a Jewish pilgrimage to Jerusalem, seen through the eyes of the young Yehoshua of Natzerat.[26] Some attempt to imagine the social location of John on first-century Patmos, its cults of Apollo and Artemis and its proximity to mainland cities such as Miletos, can illuminate a historical study of the book of Revelation and its author.

To do

Select a section (two or three chapters) from one of the gospels, or Acts, or a letter of Paul. Pay attention to any geographical locations mentioned. Locate these places on a map, using your study Bible or a Bible atlas. How does an awareness of the geography aid your understanding?

Source Criticism

Let us look at the various methods employed by historical critics in some more detail. The first is known as *source criticism* ('criticism' is not meant to imply a negative procedure, but points to a method that 'makes judgements' (from the Greek *krinō* meaning 'I judge')). Source criticism is concerned to uncover underlying sources used by the New Testament authors. In the previous chapter we already engaged in some source criticism, when we looked at the Synoptic Problem. Solutions to the Synoptic Problem are essentially asking: what are the sources used by later gospels, such that we can account for the similarities and the differences between them? In the common solutions, it is believed that we possess at least one of the written sources of the later gospels (Mark if the Two Source Theory is correct; Matthew and Luke if the Griesbach Hypothesis is preferred; Mark and Matthew for the Farrer Hypothesis).

Source criticism is not confined to the synoptic gospels, however. Though more difficult (given that we do not possess any of these extant sources), many believe that a Signs Source underlies John's Gospel. Verbatim agreements in certain passages between Colossians and Ephesians, or between Jude and 2 Peter, have led source critics to ask whether one of these is the source for the other. Study of Acts has sometimes attempted to reconstruct the sources used by Luke in composing his second volume.

The following criteria have often been used by source critics in order to detect and isolate underlying sources in a text:

- *Verbatim agreement (or near agreement) between two texts:* this is the case especially in synoptic study, where shared content and closeness in wording seems to point to one version being the source for another.
- *Doublets:* when the same saying, or similar material, is found twice in the same book, source critics have seen this as evidence for the combination of two sources. One such doublet in Mark is the similar sequence of stories beginning with a sea miracle and ending with a feeding miracle (Mark 4.35—6.44; 6.45—8.10). Though paralleled in Matthew, the whole second sequence is omitted by Luke.
- *Inconsistencies:* inconsistencies and other 'rough seams' in the text are treated as evidence for the editing of different sources. In Mark 6.45, for

example, Jesus gets into a boat and makes for Bethsaida; at 6.53, however, he lands not at Bethsaida but at Gennesaret. Source critics would conclude that inconsistent combining of sources accounts for this discrepancy.

- *Mixed literary forms:* for example, when a prose letter seems to move into poetic or hymnic form, or a discursive letter suddenly changes to the densely packed wording normally associated with a creed. Many believe, for example, that imbedded in the Pauline letters there are fragments of early Christian creeds (for example, Romans 1.3–4; 3.24–5; 1 Thessalonians 1.9–10), as well as a number of hymns (for example, Philippians 2.6–11; Colossians 1.15–20).

Source criticism is often illuminating, especially when comparing two or more of the synoptic gospels. As an example, let us take the story of plucking grain on the sabbath (Matthew 12.1–8 and parallels; Aland §46; Throckmorton §69):

Matthew 12.1–8	*Mark 2.23–8*	*Luke 6.1–5*
At that time Jesus went through the cornfields on the sabbath; his disciples were hungry, and they began to pluck heads of grain and to eat. When the Pharisees saw it, they said to him,	One sabbath he was going through the cornfields; and as they made their way his disciples began to pluck heads of grain. The Pharisees said to him,	One sabbath while Jesus was going through the cornfields, his disciples plucked some heads of grain, *rubbed them in their hands*, and ate them. But some of the Pharisees said,
'Look, your disciples are doing what is not lawful to do on the sabbath.'	'Look, why are they doing what is not lawful on the sabbath?'	'Why are you doing what is not lawful on the sabbath?'
He said to them, 'Have you not read what David did when he and his	And he said to them, 'Have you never read what David did, when he and his	Jesus answered, 'Have you not read what David did when he and his

Matthew 12.1–8	*Mark 2.23–8*	*Luke 6.1–5*
companions were hungry?	companions were hungry and in need of food?	companions were hungry?
He entered the house of God and	He entered the house of God, *when Abiathar was high priest,*	He entered the house of God,
ate the bread of the Presence, which it was not lawful for him or his companions to eat, but only for the priests?	and ate the bread of the Presence, which it is not lawful for any but	and took and ate the bread of the Presence, which it was not lawful for any but the priests to eat, and gave some to his companions?'
	the priests to eat, and he gave some to his companions.'	
Or have you not read in the law that on the sabbath the priests in the temple break the sabbath, and yet are guiltless? I tell you, something greater than the temple is here. But if you had known what this means, 'I desire mercy and not sacrifice,' you would not have condemned the guiltless.		
		Then he said to them,
	Then he said to them, 'The sabbath was made for humankind, and not humankind for the sabbath;*	
For the Son of Man is lord of the sabbath.'	*sabbath;* so the Son of Man is lord *even* of the sabbath.'	'The Son of Man is lord of the sabbath.'

The underlined words denote where there is verbatim agreement between all three versions (there is occasionally also verbatim agreement between two where the third diverges). The words in italics represent substantial wording that is unique to one of the three. What might a source critic make of this passage?

- The large amount of verbatim agreement makes it highly likely that one of the gospels is the source here for the other two.
- The variations between the accounts has suggested to most scholars that the most likely solution is that this source is Mark's Gospel.
- One reason for this is that Mark is the middle term between the two. When Matthew or Luke diverges from Mark, the other follows Mark. For example, where Luke has 'Why are you doing . . .', Mark and Matthew have 'why are they [Matthew 'your disciples'] doing . . .?' Mark and Luke agree in the words 'which it was not lawful *for any but the priests to eat*', while Matthew diverges at this point. As the Griesbach Hypothesis argues, however, the fact that Mark is the middle term need not mean that Mark is the first, but could also be accounted for by Mark being the third.
- The substantial extra material in Matthew's version (about the priests profaning the sabbath etc.) is also best accounted for by Matthew using Mark as a source. It is unlikely that Mark and Luke would both have omitted this material if it were present in their only source for this story. On the other hand, it is an explicable Matthean addition, to rule out Jesus being understood as a lawbreaker.
- The addition found in Luke ('rubbing them in their hands') is also better explained as a Lucan addition to his source, explaining how they got at the grain kernels.
- One can make better sense of the omission of the additional Marcan material in Matthew and Luke on the grounds of Marcan priority, rather than Mark expanding his source. 'When Abiathar was high priest' is factually incorrect: it was Abiathar's father Ahimelech who was high priest when this episode occurred (1 Samuel 21.1–6). Matthew and Luke knew their Old Testament better than Mark, so omitted his mistake. They could both have omitted the Marcan saying 'The sabbath was made for

man . . .' because it appeared too extreme an interpretation of the sabbath, or because it might imply that human beings generally, rather than the unique Son of man Jesus, are lords of the sabbath.

- Finally, a source critic might also notice other minor agreements between Matthew and Luke against Mark: these are not simply the shared omissions just mentioned, but shared additions to the wording (for example, 'not lawful *to do* on the sabbath'; 'Have you *never* read . . .?'). These are problematic for the Q hypothesis, suggesting that there is some literary relationship also between Matthew and Luke.

Source criticism is relatively easy when we have two or more texts to compare (as with the synoptic gospels). It is much more difficult, however, and increasingly hypothetical, when we do not. This is particularly the case with a gospel like John, where the evangelist has so skilfully reworked sources into a coherent theological vision that they are now very difficult to separate out. It equally holds for attempts to uncover Mark's sources (if Mark is indeed the first gospel). The following criticisms have been made of source criticism:

- The presumption of many of the criteria is that sources can only be detected when an author/editor has done a botch job (for example, left 'rough seams' or other inconsistencies in the text).
- It is often very difficult to separate out tradition and redaction (can we be sure that so-called Marcan 'style' was not in Mark's source, for example?).
- A feature like repetition may be there for dramatic effect, rather than evidence for shoddy combination of different sources. It may well serve Mark's (and Matthew's) purposes to have two feeding miracles, for example, one on Jewish soil to symbolize the feeding of Israel, one in the Decapolis to point to the spread of the kingdom to the non-Jewish world.
- Similarly, one person's 'inconsistency' is another person's 'literary technique'. A greater appreciation of the literary skill of New Testament authors means that scholars are less willing than previously to attribute all unusual features to the combination of different sources.

Nevertheless, used judiciously, source criticism can help locate the texts in some kind of chronological sequence, and point to passages which provide glimpses into earlier Christian practice and beliefs.

> **To do**
>
> Compare the following sets of texts. What questions might a source critic ask of them? Can you decide whether there is likely to be a literary relationship between them, and if so, which is the source for the other?
> * Matthew 14.22–33 and Mark 6.45–52
> * Ephesians 6.21–2 and Colossians 4.7–9
> * 2 Peter 3.1–4 and Jude 17–19

Between Jesus and the New Testament Writings

Source criticism has pointed to existing traditions and sources in the period prior to the writing of the New Testament books. Paul's letters point to creeds and hymns; the gospels have made use of sources about Jesus, both oral and written. Uncovering some of these has given us tantalizing glimpses into that formative period between Jesus and the written records. Most interesting is the period prior to the written gospels (*c.* late 60s to 90s). Besides what can be gleaned from source criticism, the authentic letters of Paul (dated to the early to late 50s) are themselves useful windows onto the period. The Acts of the Apostles also describes this period: it needs to be read judiciously, however, given that it was probably written late in the century, looking back on the early events from that later perspective.

The picture we glean from these sources is of a formative period in which traditions were reshaped in a number of contexts and for different purposes: prayer, liturgy, scriptural exegesis in the light of Jesus, teaching and preaching, addressing ethical issues, the need to apply Jesus' words to new situations. In 1 Corinthians 7.12–16, for example, Paul has to apply Jesus' saying about divorce to a very different scenario from Jewish Palestine: a mixed marriage between a pagan and a spouse who had become a Christian. We can learn a lot from how Paul reaches his conclusions on this pressing pastoral issue.

In fact, a number of factors are at play in this 'in-between' period, which would influence the development of the Jesus tradition prior to the writing of the first gospel:

- The spread of the gospel to diverse locations (for example, Galilee, Antioch, Ephesus, Corinth, Rome), by different preachers (for example, Peter, Paul, Apollos): this is likely to have created diverse forms of the Jesus tradition.
- The different ethnic make-up of Christian communities: Palestinian Jews; Greek-speaking Jews; other Greeks; pagans of all kinds. Particular stories would have had particular relevance to certain groups (for example, Jesus' debates over legal observance for Christians from a Jewish background; the story of the Syro-Phoenician woman for Gentile converts).
- The reapplication of stories in the tradition (in preaching and teaching), to provide new or deeper meanings or lessons. The story about Jesus eating with (Jewish) tax-collectors and sinners, for example, may well have been reused to justify the Church's admission of Gentile outsiders (whether Jewish and Gentile Christians could eat together was a live issue in the early Church: Galatians 2.11–14).
- The change of language, from Aramaic (in which the bulk of Jesus' teaching was most likely spoken) to Greek. As we saw in Chapter 4, translation from one language to another throws up a host of interpretative issues.
- Cultural factors, related to the diverse locations and audiences: these have left their mark on the written gospels: Mark, for example, needs to explain distinctive Jewish practices, whereas Matthew assumes his audiences will know what a phylactery is; the fact that Luke calls the Sea of Galilee 'the lake' suggests that his world is that of the Mediterranean (he knows what a real sea is!).
- The development of beliefs about Jesus (particularly as Christianity moved out of a strict monotheism): this affected the way Jesus was described in the tradition, or how stories about him were told.

Form Criticism

Form criticism (from the German *Formgeschichte* or 'the history of form') is especially interested in this 'in-between' period in which the tradition was developing. It was first applied to the gospels by early twentieth-century German scholars: Karl Ludwig Schmidt, Martin Dibelius and Rudolf Bultmann.[27] Looking at Mark, believed to be the earliest gospel, the form critics noticed that – with the notable exception of the passion narrative, which was a coherent, connected sequence of events – the individual units (technically called *pericope* from the Greek meaning 'cut around') were rather loosely connected. In other words, they concluded, the various stories and sayings probably circulated independently at the oral stage, without particular chronological or geographical setting. In fact, the concerns of the form critics were fourfold:

- To isolate the individual units or *pericopae* from their present context in the gospel narratives.
- To classify them according to literary form (for example, miracle story, parable).
- To establish their likely *Sitz im Leben* or 'setting in life', both in the life of the Church (the context within which such a story was told and shaped: for example, liturgy, preaching, teaching of converts) and in the life of Jesus (though some form critics rather sceptically concluded that certain stories were 'creations' of the early Church).
- To ask how these forms developed, by identifying layers of interpretation.

Luke Johnson offers a helpful analogy to the conviction of the form critics that the Jesus tradition would have assumed typical forms. He imagines a family remembering its deceased matriarch. When family members met together, especially for holiday celebrations or other ritual occasions, they would reminisce, tell stories about her characteristic behaviour and sayings, and engage in mutual correction of each other's memories (at least while eyewitnesses were still alive). Over time, these 'Grandma' stories would develop into set forms, and could be classified according to type:

for example, 'Arguing with Grandpa' stories; 'Advice to the Grandchildren' stories; 'Grandma's One-Liners'. Not all of these would be linked to a specific occasion or location.[28]

Form critics believe that a similar process happened with the Jesus tradition. Hence, as the oral tradition developed, Jesus sayings and stories about Jesus' deeds fell into set stereotypical forms, comparable to forms found elsewhere in the Jewish and classical world. These were circulated independently, often in oral form. There is some New Testament evidence that this is no mere hypothesis: independent sayings of or stories about Jesus are found in Paul's letters (for example, 1 Corinthians 7.10–11; 9.14; 11.23–5; 1 Thessalonians 5.2), one more is mentioned in Acts (Acts 20.35), while parallels to Matthew's Sermon on the Mount are found in the letter of James.

Different forms were used and retold for different purposes. The miracle stories, for example, seem to have been told to authenticate Jesus as the one acting on God's behalf. Sometimes, stories seem to contain 'mixed forms': the healing of the paralytic man (Mark 2.1–12 and parallels), for example, was viewed by Bultmann as the combination of a miracle story with the saying about forgiveness (hence provoking controversy).[29] The healing of the centurion's servant (Matthew 8.5–13 = Luke 7.1–10) is a miracle story which appears to have been reworked so that, in its present form, it compares the faith of a Gentile centurion favourably with that of Israel (perhaps justifying the Gentile mission).

There is some variation in the names given to particular forms (for example, Bultmann's 'apophthegms' were called by Dibelius 'paradigms', while the British scholar Vincent Taylor called them 'pronouncement stories'). Moreover, there is debate as to whether the shorter is necessarily the earlier: did the tradition start with 'pure' forms which accumulated interpretation as it was passed on, rather like a snowball? Or should we rather think of the pericopae as like pebbles being smoothed by the sea: in other words, longer stories were gradually 'smoothed' and abbreviated into set forms at a later stage? Or did both processes happen, in which case each pericope needs to be considered on its own merits?

Form criticism tended to view the New Testament authors, especially the evangelists, as essentially collators of tradition. Mark, for example, has done little more than string together various units of tradition 'like pearls

---

Table 6: Some Literary Forms.

- *Pronouncement stories* (including conflict stories, focusing on Jesus' 'punch line')
- *Miracle stories* (subdivided into healings, exorcisms, nature miracles)
- *Parables* (including proverbs, similes and detailed stories)
- *Legends* (for example, Jesus' baptism; the temptation; the transfiguration)
- *Genealogies* (for example, the genealogies of Jesus in Matthew 1 and Luke 3)
- *Liturgy* (for example, creeds, hymns and canticles, confessions)

---

on a string' (the 'string' being his narrative summaries, connecting phrases such as 'and immediately', and the occasional time and place reference). The real interest is in the prehistory of the units of gospel tradition, in what context they would have been shaped and told, rather than in the gospels themselves.

To do

Read Mark 1—2. Try to isolate the different units of tradition, and identify their various literary forms. Is it possible to detect Mark's editing of these units?

Redaction Criticism

Redaction criticism, while building upon source and form criticism, represents something of a reaction to undue focus on the prehistory of the New Testament text. Like its predecessors, it has been applied particularly to the study of the gospels. Far from treating the evangelists as mere compilers of tradition, redaction critics give more space to the creative editing or *redaction* of the evangelist's sources. Not content with identifying units of tradition, they ask *why* the evangelist has chosen these particular units rather than others, and why they have been put together in this particular order. Redaction critics also pay attention to detailed changes made by an evangelist to his sources (for example, Luke's alterations of Mark). When applied on a broad scale (as opposed to the micro scale), it is sometimes known as *composition criticism*, because of its interest in the overall composition of the work. Both redaction and composition criticism are concerned with the new meanings created by the coming together of traditional sources and the gospel authors.

Classic redaction-critical works include Bornkamm, Barth and Held on Matthew, Marxsen on Mark, and Conzelmann on Luke.[30] Morna Hooker's perceptive comment on the form critics' 'pearls on a string' analogy provides a flavour of redaction criticism's renewed focus on the creativity of the evangelists as authors and theologians in their own right:

> It will not, I hope, be regarded as a sexist remark if I suggest that only a man could have used the phrase 'like pearls on a string' to suggest a haphazard arrangement of material. Any woman would have spotted at once the flaw in the analogy: pearls need to be carefully selected and graded. And gradually it has dawned on New Testament scholars that this is precisely what the evangelists have done with their material. Their arrangements are anything but haphazard. The stories may not be in order chronologically – but they most certainly have an order.[31]

Closer attention to the order of Mark's Gospel bears out her point. A series of controversy stories in Mark 2.1—3.6, for example, heightens the sense of growing opposition to Jesus from a range of religious groups (the scribes, the scribes of the Pharisees, 'some people', the Pharisees, the Pharisees and Herodians). Many redaction critics have noticed Mark's 'sandwich' technique, whereby one pericope is 'sandwiched' between the two halves of a second. The two interwoven stories mutually interpret each other. Thus in Mark 3.20–35, the story about the scribes accusing Jesus of demon possession is sandwiched between his family (or 'neighbours') thinking he is out of his mind (3.20–1) and his mother and brothers standing outside (3.31–5). The healing of the woman with a 12-year-old haemorrhage is sandwiched between two parts of the raising of Jairus' daughter, herself 12 years old, as if a model of faith for Jairus to imitate (5.21–43). The cleansing of the 'barren' temple is sandwiched between the cursing and withering of the barren fig tree (11.12–26).

Redaction critics will typically look out for the following features:

- *The changing of the order of events, or the setting of a story*: for example, Luke recounts Jesus' preaching in the Nazareth synagogue before any other story of Jesus' public ministry (even delaying the call of the first disciples), stressing the importance of this episode for understanding who Jesus is.
- *The use of two sources*: for example, when Matthew and Luke combine the triple tradition parable of the Mustard Seed with the double tradition parable of the Leaven; or when Matthew has two different versions of the saying about divorce (does repetition point to it being an important theme for him?).
- *The insertion of new material*: for example, Matthew's additional material about Peter in the story of the Walking on the Water and the Caesarea Philippi episode (Matthew 14.22–33; 16.13–20).
- *The altering of details*: for example, Luke has the last two temptations in a different order to Matthew in his version of Jesus' temptation in the wilderness (Luke 4.5–12). Many think he has done this to highlight his emphasis upon Jerusalem and the Temple.

To do

Look back at the parallel accounts of eating grain on the sabbath. What are the differences between Matthew's account and the other two? what difference do they make? What do you think Matthew was trying to say through his additional material?

Actual Archaeology

We started this chapter by likening historical approaches to the New Testament, especially the gospels, to an archaeological dig. But does actual archaeology also have anything to contribute to historical understanding of the New Testament? Some scholars are understandably suspicious of relying too much on archaeology, given the way in which sensationalist claims are regularly made: either that archaeology has 'undermined the New Testament' or that it has 'proved' its historical accuracy.

However, there are three reasons why archaeology is an important component in historical reading of the New Testament. First, it helps give us a better *general* picture of the world in which Jesus and the New Testament writers lived, its cultural diversity, and its similarities to and differences from our own world. The discovery and interpretation of artefacts from the Roman Mediterranean, including Roman Palestine, and the excavation of ancient towns and cities, help put flesh on the bare bones of what we know about this period from written sources.

Second, archaeology can shed light on *specific* locations mentioned in the New Testament, and thereby on the emerging Christian communities living there. The excavation of villas and temples in Roman Corinth, for example, has helped our understanding of why two issues arose among Paul's Corinthian Christians: divisions at the Eucharist (because they met in houses, which were limited in space), and debates about eating meat sacrificed to idols (the city was full of temples, many of which contained dining rooms). Detailed excavations of Herodian Jerusalem have enabled scholars to reconstruct the city as it would have been in the first century (a fine example is the model in the gardens of Jerusalem's Holy Land Hotel).

Finally, archaeological finds can sometimes provide datings to events mentioned in the New Testament, or provide external evidence for the existence of figures mentioned in it. The discovery of a dated inscription at Delphi in Greece, mentioning Lucius Iunius Gallio as proconsul of Achaia (the so-called 'Gallio Inscription'), enables scholars to date Paul's first stay in Corinth with some degree of accuracy, for this Gallio is also mentioned in Acts (Acts 18.12).

To do

Using Bible dictionaries, and internet resources, find out as much as possible about the following: the Erastus inscription; the Caiaphas ossuary; the Via Egnatia. What light might these shed on the New Testament?

Further Reading

Rudolf Bultmann, 1963, *The History of the Synoptic Tradition,* ET Oxford: Basil Blackwell.

Eric Franklin, 1982, *How the Critics Can Help*, London: SCM Press.

J. L. Houlden (ed.), 1995, *The Interpretation of the Bible in the Church*, London: SCM Press, especially pp. 7–19.

Edgar V. McKnight, 1969, *What is Form Criticism?* Philadelphia: Fortress Press.

Norman Perrin, 1969, *What is Redaction Criticism?* Philadelphia: Fortress Press.

7

Literary Readings

Looking at a Tapestry

In Chapter 5, we spoke about the canonical gospels as four 'portraits' of Jesus, each presenting him from a different perspective in order to elicit a particular response from the reader or hearer. Just as one can view different portraits of the same subject in an art gallery such as London's National Gallery, so one can 'view' four Jesus portraits by reading the New Testament. Redaction criticism is especially interested in the 'portraits' provided by individual writers (although being a historical approach, it asks further questions such as why the writer wrote in this particular way, and what was going on in the writer's time which might account for this perspective).

However, one might enter a room in an art gallery and, instead of encountering a series of portraits, be brought face to face with a vast canvas or a large tapestry. This larger scale enables a much bigger picture to be seen at once. Annibale Carracci's *Landscape with the Flight into Egypt*, in the Doria Pamphilj Gallery in Rome (www.doriapamphilj.it/ukfuga.asp), locates this gospel scene against a broad rural landscape, encouraging us to imagine the before and after of this moment in the Holy Family's journey. Tapestries offer something even greater. They often contain several scenes, allowing these to be viewed simultaneously and in relation to each other. They are also magnificently produced: their coloured threads woven together in an intricate way to produce different images, textures and recurring patterns. The set of fourteenth-century tapestries of the book of Revelation, now housed in Angers castle in France, is a dramatic example of how an intricate book like the Apocalypse can be presented in visual form (a web search will reveal a large number of websites devoted to these magnificent tapestries).

The image of the tapestry is a useful one to describe the recent shift towards more holistic, literary approaches to the New Testament. These urge us to read a book as a whole, paying attention to how the constitutive parts fit together, rather like the bird's-eye view of several scenes afforded by a tapestry. They also pay attention to the highs and lows in the narrative flow (like the different textures in the tapestry), and the way in which themes are repeated and interwoven as the book progresses (like the recurrence and interweaving of a tapestry's coloured threads).

Critique of Historical Criticism

This range of newer literary approaches has drawn upon and learnt from developments in secular literary studies. Though literary approaches are essentially positive, they have become popular in part due to a growing recognition of the limitations of historical-critical methods (for example, source, form and redaction criticism). Whereas historical criticism is essentially *diachronic* (taking us 'through time' to the historical circumstances of the New Testament authors, and further back to the sources and traditions used), these literary approaches are *synchronic* ('same time', focusing on the text in its final form). Some of the main areas of dissatisfaction literary critics have with historical-critical methods are as follows:

- Historical criticism (especially source and form criticism) seems more concerned with the prehistory of earlier traditions than the text itself. Even redaction criticism, while interested in the human author's overall message, nevertheless focuses on that author rather than the text the author produced.
- The tendency of historical critics is to chop the text up, rather than treat it holistically. The New Testament books are handled like a piece of meat on a butcher's slab, or a corpse in a post-mortem examination. Take a text, dissect it to see what the various parts look like (and then interpret reconstructed sources: for example, the Johannine Signs Source; the hypothetical source Q).

- As has already been mentioned, some scholars question how far, if at all, the authorial intention of New Testament writings (especially the gospels) is recoverable.

Mark Allen Powell, a noted literary critic who nonetheless recognizes the benefits of historical approaches, puts it this way:

> As a literary critic, I have concerns about a hermeneutic (that is, an approach to interpretation) that privileges so exclusively the value of authorial intent. Any literature that is worth reading transcends the contextual interests specific to its production.[32]

In reaction to such criticisms, literary approaches (especially that branch known as *narrative criticism*, which is discussed in more detail below) represent the following shifts in study of the New Testament:

- *From author to text and reader:* the focus is not on the historical author of, for example, Matthew's Gospel, but on the text produced by that author, and on the impact of that text upon the contemporary reader.
- *From sources and prehistory to final text:* rather than chopping up the text and examining its constitutive parts, literary criticism examines the finished product, the final form in its entirety. In practice, there will be differences as to what the 'final form' is (which ending of Mark should be considered, for example? Should the story of the woman taken in adultery be treated as an integral part of John? Should one attend to the Greek, or work with an English translation?). The three-year Sunday lectionary cycle used by many churches (the Roman Lectionary; the ecumenical Revised Common Lectionary; the Church of England's slightly different Common Worship Lectionary) encourages this kind of holistic reading of the synoptic gospels: they are organized according to a year of Matthew, a year of Mark and a year of Luke.
- *From history to narrative:* literary critics place less emphasis upon historical reconstruction in favour of an appreciation of texts as narratives. This is especially the case with the gospels and Acts; but also possibly the epistles and Revelation. Katherine Grieb's recent book on Romans, for example, offers an illuminating reading in which Paul retells a series of interlocking

stories.[33] In contrast to being a compendium of Pauline theology, Romans recounts the story of humanity, and within that the story of Israel, and within that the story of Christ, and within that the story of those – both Jew and Gentile – who are in Christ in Rome.

While literary approaches have highlighted the limitations of historical criticism, they have not been without their critics. Purely literary approaches may gloss over some of the difficulties or tensions that historical study raises, for example (such as differences between evangelists; differences in cultural assumptions). As a result, many scholars consider rumours of the demise of historical criticism premature. Nevertheless, holistic readings based on close study of the text and its emotional impact deserve a valued place in any attempt to understand and respond to the New Testament. Not least this is a recognition that some of the texts may have been intended to be read in a single instalment. Those who have witnessed the one-man performances of Mark's Gospel by Alec McCowan or Dawson Peters will appreciate the powerful impact of hearing a gospel at one sitting.

Reflection

Reflect on what you have learned so far about historical-critical approaches to the New Testament. What are its benefits? Do you agree with all or any of the above criticisms? If not, why not? Are there other criticisms you have which are not listed here?

Narrative Criticism

One of the most commonly used literary approaches is narrative criticism. As just noted, this has been applied especially to obvious narratives such as the gospels and Acts, though it is arguably of use for interpreting other New Testament books. Whereas historical approaches tend to ask about 'the world behind the text' (for example, why did Matthew write as he did? was there an earlier form of Luke's Magnificat?), narrative critics are interested in 'the world of the text'. This does not mean that narrative critics *necessarily* think that historical questions are unimportant. However, they tend to bracket such questions off in favour of other interests. Insofar as they ask questions about the readers (real or implied), they are also interested in 'the world in front of the text', namely, the engagement between text and reader.

Narrative criticism can be viewed as one form of what is known as *reader-response criticism*. As its name suggests, reader-response criticism is interested in the responses of modern readers to the text, the dynamic interplay between reader and text. For some reader-response critics – including narrative critics – the text places particular constraints on interpretation. Hence, they are interested in how the text influences the reader. Other reader-response critics are more interested in the creative role of each individual reader in responding to the text and creating meaning in that encounter (Chapter 9 will look in more detail at the role of readers in the process of interpretation).

In particular, narrative critics are interested in the following:

- *Implied Author:* since little may be certain about the actual author of a New Testament text (for example, name, background, place and date of writing), narrative critics speak instead of the implied author, the author as implied by the text. That is, the picture gleaned from clues in the text as to the kind of person who would have written it. The implied author of Revelation, for example, would be a Jewish Christian prophet called John (probably a Semitic speaker given the quality of his written Greek), who received visions while an exile on Patmos. This holds whether or not the book was actually written by a John who had been on Patmos, and even if we can't be sure whether he is to be identified with John the son of Zebedee or 'John the presbyter' (one of the big debates in Revelation studies). In the case of letters like 1 Timothy and 2 Peter, many scholars are persuaded that the implied authors (the apostles Paul and Peter) are different individuals from the actual authors (these letters are believed to be *pseudonymous*, from the Greek 'falsely named').
- *Implied Reader* (sometimes called the *ideal reader*): the kind of person who always understands and responds to the text in the way that it seems to imply an attentive reader should. In Kingsbury's words, the implied reader responds to the text 'with whatever emotion, understanding, or

knowledge the text ideally calls for'.[34] For example, the implied reader of Matthew would be a Jewish Christian, who understands what phylacteries are for, is sympathetic (at least by the end of the narrative) towards the Gentile mission, and has a negative attitude towards the Pharisees as characters in the story.

- *Shape of the Narrative:* narrative critics attend to a text's structure, and connections between its various parts. This includes paying attention to 'textual markers', points in a text where an author seems to particularly come to the fore: for example, passing a comment on the action, providing a conclusion or a summary, offering a temporal transition (for example, 'Two months later . . .'). Francis Moloney, for example, plots out the following basic structure for Mark's Gospel on the basis of what he regards as four clear textual markers (at 1.1; 1.14–15; 8.31; 16.1–4):[35]

Mark 1.1–13 (Prologue)
Mark 1.14—8.30 (Jesus' Galilean ministry, culminating in Peter's confession)
Mark 8.31—15.47 (Jesus' movement towards Jerusalem, and his ministry there)
Mark 16.1–8 (Discovery of the empty tomb)

This initial structural outline – highlighting dramatic turning points in the narrative – provides the basis on which he can further subdivide the narrative (for example, the fast-moving action in Mark 1.14—8.30 is 'slowed down' in places by summaries of Jesus' deeds which introduce new subsections: 1.14—3.6; 3.7—6.6a; 6.6b—8.30).

- *Plot:* there is interest in the way in which the story unfolds and the plot develops (following clues in the text). So, whereas redaction critics would tend to point to the five teaching-blocks or discourses (Matthew 5—7, 10, 13, 18 and 24—25) as important for understanding Matthew's structure, narrative critics would tend to focus on the unfolding drama (for example, the growing opposition to Jesus).
- *Setting:* both the temporal (for example, 'The next day') and the geographical setting are considered significant. For example, when Mark's Jesus moves from the synagogue (where he experiences hostility, Mark 3.1–6) to the seaside (where the crowds are generally receptive, Mark 3.7–12), narrative

critics often regard these two settings as symbolic of different responses to him. Similarly, the two sides of the Sea of Galilee (for example, Mark 4.35—5.1) may symbolize the Jewish and Gentile missions respectively.

- *Characterization:* attention to the characters or actors as created by the author, paying attention to their role within the world of the story (narrative critics stress that these may or may not approximate to actual historical figures: for example, actual Pharisees). Some narrative critics call the characters/actors 'actants', because they may include non-humans such as animals or angels. Particular attention is paid to how the narrative encourages the implied readers to respond to specific characters or groups of characters: do they inspire *empathy* (a desire to identify with them: for example, Jesus himself, or the centurion whose faith is praised), or more distant *sympathy* (for example, Nicodemus in John 3), or *antipathy* (for example, the magician Elymas in Acts 13)?
- *Point of View:* how the implied reader responds to these characters is related to the implied author's point of view manifesting itself in the text. This may come through explicitly (for example, when Mark says of Jesus: 'Thus he declared all foods clean', Mark 7.19b), or be implicit in the text.
- *Literary Techniques:* for example, the use of irony, or symbolism by the implied author to encourage the implied reader to reject certain interpretations and accept others. For example, there is irony in the mocking acclamation of Jesus as 'king of the Jews' by the soldiers at Mark 15.16–20 (the implied reader knows that Jesus really is king of the Jews!). When Jesus speaks to his disciples of having 'food to eat that you do not know about' (John 4.32), he is speaking symbolically of doing the Father's will. The implied reader has been attuned by the narrative to be sensitive to such deeper meanings. Other narrative patterns are listed in Table 7.
- *Narrative Time:* the use of time in the narrative is significant. Sometimes it is slowed down, in order to point to an event's significance (for example, the comparative length of time devoted to the last hours of Jesus' earthly life), sometimes speeded up (for example, the 'rush' of the beginning of Jesus' ministry in Mark). Sometimes, events are recounted out of narrative time: e.g. the beheading of John the Baptist in Matthew and Mark is told as a 'flashback', perhaps heralding what is to happen to Jesus, and to those sent out in his name.

Table 7: Some Narrative Patterns.

- *Repetition* (for example, John 14 and 16; three accounts in Acts of Paul's Damascus Road experience);
- *Climax* (for example, Peter's confession in Mark 8)
- *Inclusio* (two parallel elements bracketing a section of text: e.g. Matthew 1.23 'God is with us' and 28.20: 'I am with you always')
- *Chiasm* (an A, B, B, A pattern: e.g. Jesus' saying at Mark 2.27).
- *Concentric patterns* (an A, B, C, B, A pattern, where the centre plays a crucial role: e.g. Sermon on the Mount (Matthew 5—7), centred on the Lord's Prayer)

To do

Read (or ask someone else to read to you) Luke's account of the Gerasene demoniac (Luke 8.26–39). Whom do you identify with in the story? Do you feel sympathy or antipathy to any other characters? Why might this be? Try changing roles, and ask whether you are hearing the story differently.

Putting it into Practice

In order to put this into practice, let us attempt a narrative reading of the healing of the centurion's servant in Matthew 8.5–13. This means that we will put on one side the historical questions (for example, what was the original form of this story, which is also found in Luke 7.1–10 and very similar to a story in John 4.46–54; how do we account for the differences between Matthew and Luke?). What kind of questions and conclusions might arise from such a reading?

- Its *context* in the unfolding narrative is significant: it is the second of a collection of miracles (Matthew 8—9), which follow on from the portrayal of Jesus as an authoritative teacher in the Sermon on the Mount (Matthew 5—7). Is the implied reader to view this section as presenting Jesus as also powerful in deed (perhaps like Moses)? Some might see the selection of the first three miracles as especially significant: they concern people either on (a leper, a woman) or beyond (a Roman centurion) the margins of Israel's society.
- In terms of its *literary structure*, the story has a concentric structure, giving Jesus' praise of the centurion's faith central importance (thus emphasizing the *point of view* of the *implied author*):

A situation of servant/boy (verses 5–6)
  B Jesus' word offering to heal (verse 7)
    C centurion's declaration of unworthiness (verses 8–9)
      D Jesus praises centurion's faith (verse 10)
    C´ promise of reversal in the kingdom (verses 11–12)
  B´ Jesus' word effecting the healing (verse 13a)
A´ changed situation of servant/boy (verse 13b)

- Some might see significance in the geographical *setting* of the incident. Capernaum (verse 5) has only been mentioned once before in Matthew: at Matthew 4.13–15, we learn that Capernaum, the chosen centre of Jesus' ministry, is in 'Galilee of the Gentiles'. Might this earlier association of Capernaum with Gentiles have prepared the way, however implicitly, for the positive portrayal of a Gentile here?
- Of the *characters* in the story, the implied reader will surely feel empathy towards Jesus. The centurion also ought to inspire empathy (at least in the light of the whole story), whereas Israel, including Jesus' Jewish disciples, can inspire at best sympathy, for deficiency in faith (verse 10).
- Nevertheless, we should not underestimate the story's potential shock value for the implied reader, for at least two reasons. First, if the Greek word *pais* is translated as 'servant' or 'servant-boy' rather than 'child', the implied reader (familiar with the Jewish tradition) might be troubled about the precise relationship between him and the centurion, with a pos-

sible hint of sexual innuendo.[36] Second, given Jesus' words in verse 10, this centurion is a pagan. There is no indication here (unlike Luke's parallel account) that he worships the God of Israel rather than the gods of Rome. He has simply expressed his faith or trust in Jesus' ability to heal.

- The *implied reader* is sufficiently familiar with the Jewish tradition to understand the phrase 'sons of the kingdom' as referring to Jews, the descendants of the patriarchs. Again, there is shock in the radical reversal implied in verses 11–12, whereby places at the table in the kingdom are given to outsiders, whose own place is taken by former insiders.

- Other *literary features* in the story also highlight this gospel reversal: the 'weeping and gnashing of teeth' phrase, with its strong note of judgement, becomes something of a refrain throughout the gospel, highlighting the theme (also Matthew 13.42, 50; 22.13; 24.51; 25.30). The use of the word *pais* for the person cured also takes on a further resonance in the context of the gospel as a whole, for Jesus is God's *pais*, who proclaims justice to the Gentiles (Matthew 12.18). Within the passage itself, the repetition of the verb 'heal' (verses 8 and 13) and the noun 'faith' (verses 10 and 13) emphasize the importance of these themes.

- The use of *narrative time* is also interesting: the narrative slows during the encounter between Jesus and the centurion, but speeds up so as to gloss over the time it would have taken for the witnesses to discover that the servant/child had been healed 'in that hour'. Again, this highlights the faith aspect rather than the miracle aspect of the story.

To do

Read Mark's account of the baptism of Jesus (Mark 1.9–11). What kind of questions might a narrative critic ask of this story? In particular, ask how it fits into its immediate context, and into the narrative as a whole. Try to detect literary links with the story of Jesus' death (Mark 15.37–9). Why might these two scenes be paralleled? It may help to know that in Greek 'the Spirit' (*pneuma*) is related to the verb 'expired' (*exepneusen*); Mark 10.38 may also be relevant.

Intertextuality

The story of the centurion's servant brings us into the realm of *intertextuality*. This approach is founded on the recognition that texts are related to one another, that subsequent authors use words and associations made possible by earlier texts. Indeed, if we use the metaphor of texts as tapestries suggested at the beginning of this chapter, the words and themes of older texts are part of the threads woven into the whole. In the New Testament, there are especially intertextual relationships with the Old Testament. However, Jewish pseudepigraphical texts, classical texts and even non-literary 'texts' such as inscriptions, monuments and coins might also need to be taken into account.

Sometimes these are conscious quotations (for example, Matthew's formula citations, such as: 'All this took place to fulfil what had been spoken by the Lord through the prophet . . .', Matthew 1.22). At other times they may be only allusions (which could be conscious or semi-conscious) or even unconscious echoes.[37] Whatever they are, they bring with them a web of associations which readers will pick up on and respond to according to their familiarity with and prior understanding of those earlier texts. The name 'Jerusalem' brings with it a host of associations, some positive, some negative, some joyous, some tragic about a particular historical city. However, there are also associations connected with a 'heavenly Jerusalem' or 'the Jerusalem above', which might be viewed as better than or a replacement for its earthly counterpart.

Sometimes, the quotation from or allusion to one particular passage may act as a trigger for the wider passage of which it is a part. When Matthew cites from Jeremiah in relation to the slaughter of the innocents (Matthew 2.18), his audience may not simply be expected to recall the quoted verse, which refers to Rachel weeping for her children. If one brings the wider passage of Jeremiah 31 into the equation, the broader theme of the return of the exiles may come into play. The weeping of Rachel is but one moment in a greater story of restoration and salvation, which for Matthew finds its climax in the story of Jesus. For a successful application of intertextuality to the Pauline letters, see Richard Hays' *Echoes of Scripture in the Letters of Paul*.[38]

However, the very process of retelling or evoking older texts leaves its mark on those texts. Changes may take place in the process (for example, the form of the quotation from Micah at Matthew 2.6), which are the explicit work of the newer author. Or an author may have seen new meaning in older words.

So back to our Matthew passage we discussed above (Matthew 8.5–13): who are the many coming 'from east and west'? A number of passages seem to be evoked here: Psalm 107.3; Isaiah 43.5; Baruch 4.37; 5.5; Zechariah 8.7. In their original context, these texts apparently refer to the ingathering of the scattered tribes of Israel in the last days. In the context of Matthew 8, however, the referents of this phrase have been transformed. No longer referring to dispersed Israelites returning to the holy land, it now describes faithful Gentiles like this centurion, who find a central place in the kingdom by a process of gospel reversal.

To do

Read the sequence of the seven bowl-plagues in Revelation 16. Now read Exodus 7—11. How do these two passages mutually interpret each other? Has Revelation transformed the meaning in any way? In both cases, from whose perspective is the action recounted, and what difference might this make?

Rhetorical Criticism

Another literary approach is *rhetorical criticism,* which is interested in the literary art of persuasion. That is, how has the author used the text in order to elicit a particular response on the part of his or her audience? If what the New Testament authors proclaim is true, they clearly have an interest in convincing others of its truthfulness. Hence, rhetorical criticism pays attention to rhetorical features in a text:

- the shape of an argument;
- the use of rhetorical questions;
- promises and threats;
- encouragement and praise;

- irony and sarcasm;
- the undermining of rival points of the view.

Given its interests, it is most applicable to New Testament letters and to speeches (for example, the speeches and sermons in Acts) embedded in the text. A useful introduction is George Kennedy's *New Testament Interpretation through Rhetorical Criticism*.[39]

Although some rhetorical critics draw upon developments in contemporary literary theory, there are ancient antecedents which would have been 'in the air' in the first century, even if the New Testament writers were not formally trained in rhetoric. One aspect of classical education was rhetoric, that is training in public speaking. Classical rhetorical handbooks have survived, associated with such names as Aristotle, Cicero and Quintilian. The classical sources tend to distinguish between three types of rhetoric, appropriate to different contexts:

- *judicial:* particularly used in a forensic context, to persuade people of someone's guilt or innocence; it is a form of rhetoric concerned with evaluating past events (for example, sections of 2 Corinthians, where Paul is defending himself against his accusers in Corinth, or the speeches of Tertullus and Paul in Acts 24);
- *deliberative:* a form of rhetoric focused on persuading an audience to pursue a particular future course (for example, the Sermon on the Mount);
- *epideictic:* from the Greek meaning 'fit for display', used in speeches that praise or blame a person or a quality, in order to persuade the audience to hold to a particular position in the present (for example, Jesus' farewell speech in John 14—17).

Aristotle also identified three types of proof to be used in rhetorical arguments of whatever kind: *ethos* ('character', which persuades an audience to trust the author or speaker, and might include that author's existing authority), *pathos* (appealing to the audience's emotional response) and *logos* (use of logical argument). Such ancient categories have been taken up by New Testament scholars. Hans Dieter Betz's commentary on Galatians in the *Hermeneia* commentary series[40] is one classic exposition of a Pauline letter using ancient rhetoric, which determines his structural analysis of the whole.

Other rhetorical critics pay less attention to particular types of ancient rhetoric (even Paul may not have had formal rhetorical training), and are more interested in the way in which authors go about persuading their audiences and readerships. How are various elements of the argument put together? Is use made of promises or threats, or both? Do literary features such as irony, metaphor and sarcasm play a role? Does the author seek to oppose or ridicule opponents?

At 1 Corinthians 4.8, for example, Paul is almost certainly using sarcasm for rhetorical effect. The Corinthians are not really rich, at the pinnacle of spiritual maturity and reigning in the kingdom of God (though they believe they are!). By his ridiculing words, Paul seeks to puncture their spiritual pride. The rhetoric of the 'message to the angel of the church in Thyatira' at Revelation 2.18–29 (interestingly, the longest of the seven messages) seeks to persuade Thyatiran Christians to dissociate from the prophetess John calls 'Jezebel'. The name-calling he engages in is itself part of the rhetoric. The letter to the Hebrews is perhaps one of the most rhetorically sophisticated New Testament writings, and full of rhetorical features.

To do

Read Hebrews 10.19–39. Try to list the various rhetorical features employed by the author. Can you work out what position the implied readers are being persuaded to adopt?

Further Reading

George A. Kennedy, 1984, *New Testament Interpretation through Rhetorical Criticism*, Chapel Hill, NC/London: University of North Carolina Press.

Francis J. Moloney, 2004, *Mark: Storyteller, Interpreter, Evangelist*, Peabody, Massachusetts: Hendrickson.

Mark Allen Powell, 1993, *What is Narrative Criticism?* London: SPCK.

Mark Allen Powell, 2001, *Chasing the Eastern Star: Adventures in Biblical Reader-Response Criticism*, Louisville, Kentucky: Westminster John Knox Press.

8

Social-Scientific Readings

Real People in Social Context

Someone browsing through scholarly introductions to the New Testament might be tempted to conclude that the early Christians were 'ideas' people. Judging by chapter headings and subheadings, they were people who spent their lives debating whether Christ was best understood by an 'Adam Christology' (he was an exalted human being) or a 'Pre-existence Christology' (he existed in heaven prior to the human life of Jesus of Nazareth), or worrying about 'proto-Gnostic redeemer myths', or whether eschatology (belief about the End) was 'realized', 'future' or 'inaugurated' (and other such complex theological ideas).

That Christians of the New Testament period were concerned about theology and right belief goes without saying. But they were also people involved in the cut and thrust of life in this world. They experienced tensions and conflicts. They had ties of family allegiance. They married and had children. They worried about the price of bread and complained about urban sanitation. They were embedded in the social realities of their world, whether the city, the village, or the empire.

Social-scientific criticism of the New Testament is concerned to tap into the social aspects of early Christian life and the texts the early Christians produced. Though anticipated in some earlier scholarship which was interested in social history (drawing upon archaeology and classical literature), it emerged on the scene of New Testament scholarship in the 1970s. Among its most famous practitioners are Bruce Malina, Jerome Neyrey, John Pilch,

Gerd Theissen, Wayne Meeks, Philip Esler and John Elliott. It does not aim to replace other historical approaches (for example, source, form and redaction criticism) or literary methods, but to complement them by adding an extra social dimension. It draws upon a range of modern social-scientific methods – such as sociology and cultural anthropology – in order to shed light on the social realities underlying the New Testament texts, and the communities out of which they came or for whom they were written. In short, social-scientific approaches reveal something of the 'flesh and blood' reality of the early Christian communities, influenced by social patterns no less than ideas. They aim to shed light on their relationships and some of their problems. They help us 'walk down the streets' of first-century Ephesus, Corinth, Capernaum and Jerusalem.

What distinguishes a social-scientific approach from mainstream historical approaches? Its tendencies can be summed up as follows:

- *A focus on 'realism' as opposed to 'idealism'*: a reaction to 'pure theology' typified in earlier New Testament scholarship. It emphasizes the close relationship between ideas and social contexts.
- *A focus on what is common, typical, as opposed to the unusual and individual* (which is the focus of history): for example, social composition, lifestyles of rich and poor, the role of the 'household'. The social sciences develop, test and refine models for understanding evidence drawn from a wide variety of human societies.
- *A focus on structures and social interaction rather than history's interest in specific events*: for example, how do ancient societies function? how might a messianic movement like early Christianity have interacted with the wider Jewish community?

Practitioners of this approach are upfront about their methods, and aware of potential weaknesses:

- Some sociologists have tended towards a reductionist account of religion as simply the product of social factors (notably Durkheim). Aware of this, Theissen and Meeks have advocated a 'functional analysis' which recognizes that theological positions are affected by social factors, without reducing them simply to those social factors.

- Social-scientific approaches have sometimes been criticized for reading too much 'between the lines' of the often fragmentary evidence about early Christianity. They need to draw as widely as possible upon contemporary sources in order to lessen this danger.
- There is a concern that such approaches anachronistically apply modern categories and models to ancient situations. The best social-scientific critics are therefore explicit about their models, and strive to test and refine them against the evidence. Indeed, they would argue that learning from the social sciences – notably cultural anthropology – actually *reduces* the danger of such anachronism.
- Social-scientific critics focus on questions which may not have been consciously in the mind of the New Testament writers. This is the case, however, with many of the questions asked by other historical and literary critics; texts prompt a host of interesting and important questions which go beyond the conscious concerns of their human authors.

Reading the Social Script

A series of recent adverts on British television have proclaimed the proud boast of HSBC to be 'the world's local bank'. One of these adverts depicts a British business man being taken out to a restaurant by his Chinese hosts. Judging by his face, he is somewhat alarmed to find eel on the menu. Eager to please his hosts, however, he polishes off the lot, only to be confronted with a succession of ever larger eels. If only he had known that what to the English – clearing your plate – is a compliment, is regarded by the Chinese as questioning their generosity! At this point, the voice-over cheerfully announces that HSBC never underestimates the importance of local knowledge.

Though sometimes accused of anachronism in the application of categories and models, social-scientific critics are in fact keenly aware of the importance of 'local knowledge' for understanding the New Testament. We may see familiar words on the page (for example, family, marriage, city, church) and think that we know precisely what they mean. After all, we all come from families, many of us marry and live in cities, and Christians go to church. But in fact the New Testament world is a foreign country, and the people it describes do not see the world quite as we ourselves do. We need to be aware of the dangers of 'ethnocentric anachronism': that is, reading back into the first century ways of viewing social realities that are inappropriate to that ancient world, but which reflect our own specific cultural world-view.

John Elliott offers a helpful analogy by quoting from a 'Code of Ethics for Travelers' drawn up by the Center for Responsible Tourism in San Anselmo, California. He suggests that this (leaving aside the occasional anachronism) reflects the kind of stance that social-scientific criticism tries to encourage modern readers to have when reading the ancient New Testament books:

Code of Ethics for Travelers

Travel in a spirit of humility and with a genuine desire to meet and talk with the local people.

Be aware of the feelings of the local people; prevent what might be offensive behavior. Photography, particularly, must respect persons.

Cultivate the habit of listening and observing rather than merely hearing and seeing or knowing all the answers.

Realize that other people may have concepts of time and thought patterns that are different from yours – not inferior, only different.

Instead of only seeing the exotic, discover the richness of another culture and way of life.

Get acquainted with local customs; respect them.

Remember that you are only one among many visitors; do not expect special privileges.

When shopping through bargaining, remember that the poorest merchant will give up a profit rather than give up his or her personal dignity.

Do not make promises to local people or to new friends that you cannot keep.

Spend time each day reflecting on your experiences in order to deepen your understanding. What enriches you may be robbing others.

You want a home away from home? Why travel?[41]

What might a modern 'visitor' to the New Testament find in this different cultural world? Cultural anthropology in particular attempts to describe such differences. An influential book by Bruce Malina, first published in 1981, is a good starting point. Malina draws insights from cultural anthropology about ancient Mediterranean culture in order to shed light on the world in which the New Testament emerged.[42] In particular, he discusses the following features, and how they help us understand the New Testament better:

- Honour and shame
- Dyadic personality
- Kinship and marriage
- Limited good
- Issues of purity

Honour was especially prized in ancient Mediterranean society, and was contrasted with *shame*. Honour describes a society's affirmation of a person's worth. It may be *ascribed*, due to who one is (Jesus' genealogies in Matthew 1 and Luke 3 point to this), or because it has been given by someone powerful (for example, God giving Jesus the 'name that is above every name' at his ascension, Philippians 2.9). Or it may be actively *acquired*, for example, by inviting people to dinner, or engaging in debate, or becoming a patron, or through business dealings. Honour is always acquired at the expense of others, in a society which was highly competitive ('agonistic' from the Greek word for 'contest'). Thus gospel stories in which Jesus overcomes his opponents in debate present him as an honourable person to an ancient reader. On the other hand, set against this honour v. shame society, aspects of the Christian gospel are all the more surprising: in the cross, Jesus' honour is achieved precisely through his submitting to that which is considered shameful (for example, Hebrews 12.2).

Unlike the northern European or North American focus on personal self-worth, introspection and individualism, the ancient Mediterranean world understood a person in terms of *dyadic personality* (from the Greek for 'twin'). One's identity is determined by one's membership of the group (for example, the family). In Malina's words: 'The dyadic personality is an individual who perceives himself and forms his self-image in terms of what others perceive and feed back to him.'[43] Thus people are defined according to the social grouping of which they are part: 'Jews do not share things in common with Samaritans' (John 4.9); 'Cretans are always liars, vicious brutes, lazy gluttons' (Titus 1.12). Social groupings rather than individuals are the primary focus of moral concerns (for example, for Paul, both *Jews* and *Gentiles* have sinned). Introspective, psychological concerns are not particularly evident in our texts.

Concepts of *kinship and marriage* in the ancient Mediterranean world also differ significantly from contemporary northern European and North American understandings. The world is divided into 'kin' (including 'fictive kin' such as clients) and 'non-kin'. The relationship with one's kin is marked by trust and even altruism; with non-kin by competitiveness. Foreigners would be considered certain enemies (this adds an extra dimension to the parable of the Good Samaritan). In such a society, males lead public lives, while females are restricted to the private sphere. Women are 'embedded' in dominant males (for example, father, brother, husband). Marriages are usually arranged; the honour and commercial interests of both families are thus brought together (giving divorce a particular aspect which differs from its associations in our culture). Bonds of affection are more likely to be between brother and sister or mother and son than between husband and wife, as is the assumption in northern Europe or North America. This is important when interpreting New Testament passages about marriage and divorce: we are not comparing like with like.

The first-century Mediterranean world was essentially a peasant society, composed of villages bound socially to pre-industrial cities. This led to the concept of the *limited good*: all goods (material like flocks or land, and non-material like honour) are believed to be limited, and always in short supply. As a consequence, one could only benefit at the expense of others, and the honourable person would not attempt to accumulate wealth, but only to preserve inherited status and goods. Patron–client relationships were one way of preserving this.

Finally, ancient Mediterranean society was concerned with issues of *purity*. Order in society was preserved through rules about what was clean and what unclean. Essentially, this was a statement of who or what was in place, and who or what out of place. It could refer to persons, animals (for example, pigs were unclean, sheep clean), inanimate objects such as cups and plates, places (for example, the temple, the holy land), and time (sacred time). In the gospels, Jesus regularly encounters people considered unclean, and therefore out of place in society (for example, lepers, the woman with an issue of blood). In Paul's letters, we see concerns to establish new rules about purity and community boundaries for a community which is no longer bound by Jewish purity laws.[44]

To do

Read the story in Mark 3.20–35. Ask yourself how insights from cultural anthropology might shed light on this passage. Pay particular attention to honour and shame; expectations associated with kinship ties; distinctions between clean and unclean. When you have written your reflections, look at Bruce J. Malina and Richard L. Rohrbaugh, 2003, *Social-Science Commentary on the Synoptic Gospels,* Minneapolis: Fortress Press, pp. 158–9.

Social Aspects of Christianity in Corinth

Two notable works of social-scientific criticism have shed light on the social setting of the churches founded by Paul, especially the church in Corinth: Wayne Meeks' *The First Urban Christians* (1983) and the collection of essays by Gerd Theissen, published in English in 1982 as *The Social Setting of Pauline Christianity.*[45] Here are three examples taken from Theissen's book, which illustrate how sociological methods might shed light on issues which emerge in 1 Corinthians.

Two Types of Apostleship

In 1 Corinthians 9 Paul alludes to his decision in Corinth (and in some other places) not to earn his living by the gospel, but to work with his own hands. On one level, this appears to be a purely theological decision, based on his understanding that the gospel is 'free of charge' (1 Corinthians 9.18). Though this could seem to go against the traditional teaching of Christ (for example, Matthew 10.10b: 'for labourers deserve their food'), Paul insists upon turning his 'right' into a 'privilege'.

Theissen, however, sees a contrast between two models of apostleship, with a socio-economic aspect. The first model, that of the itinerant Christian missionary, is truer historically to Jesus of Nazareth. It would have been developed in the political and economic instability of Herodian Palestine, where it answered the problem of subsistence by advocating begging (many of Jesus' first disciples were former fishermen or farmers who could not continue their former occupations as itinerant preachers: they couldn't easily pack up their fields or the Sea of Galilee!).

Paul, however, advocates a different model (that of 'church builder') more appropriate to the (relatively) economically affluent urban Mediterranean world, which would have had little empathy for roving beggars. Paul's own trade, moreover, was more conducive to this model: as a craftsman, he could easily carry his tools around with him. But this left Paul open to the charge that he did not act like a real apostle in allowing himself to be supported financially by the community. Theissen concludes: 'The conflict between Paul and other competing missionaries in Corinth does not arise from personal animosities. It is a conflict between different types of missionaries which displays traits independent of the individuals involved.'[46]

Idol Meat

1 Corinthians 9 is in fact just part of a lengthy discussion over whether or not the Corinthian Christians should eat meat which had been sacrificed to pagan gods (1 Corinthians 8—10). This was a pressing issue in a city like Corinth, given that much of the meat on sale in the marketplace would have been offered in sacrifice in one of the city's pagan temples. Those Paul views as 'strong' do not see a problem with eating such food, given that 'no idol in the world really exists' (1 Corinthians 8.4), while 'the weak' suffer scruples, and Paul urges that no Christian should act in such as way as to offend the conscience of a weaker brother or sister.

Commentators have often interpreted this dispute theologically, in terms of a clash of ideas: the 'strong' hold Gnostic-type views, or have been influenced by Hellenistic Jewish Wisdom speculation; or the weak are Christians from a Jewish background (Diaspora Jews often became vegetarians in order to avoid inadvertently eating meat which had been contaminated by idol worship).

Theissen again adds a social and socio-economic dimension. The 'weak' and the 'strong' are two socio-economic classes, the poor and the rich (whose socio-economic status has impacted upon their theological beliefs). In the ancient world, meat was expensive. Hence the Corinthian poor were only likely to have found it on the menu in city festivals, associated with pagan rites. The wealthy, however, would not so readily have associated meat with pagan worship, given that they could afford it as part of their regular diet. Moreover, for them to have given up eating meat would have caused them to restrict social intercourse within the city, which would have had adverse effects on their business interests or prominent positions in the city's government. Paul seems to have recognized this in his rather nuanced response to the issue. Without such prominent members, the Corinthian church would have lost important means of support, and even houses in which to meet for its liturgical assemblies.

Social Stratification

This brings us to the issue of social stratification within the Corinthian church. Theissen draws upon analyses of the social stratification of ancient societies in order to shed light on the social dimension of Christianity in Corinth. He concludes that the Corinthian church was marked by internal stratification, and that this was an important factor in some of the problems.

An illustration of how this might affect the reading of New Testament texts is provided by Theissen's interpretation of 1 Corinthians 1.26–9. An older, rather romantic idea (associated, for example, with Adolf Deissman) is that the early Church was composed almost exclusively of slaves and other members of the lower social classes. On a first reading, 1 Corinthians seems to confirm this:

Consider your own call, brothers and sisters: not many of you were wise by human standards, not many were powerful, not many were of noble birth. (1 Corinthians 1.26)

However, analysing this verse in the light of sociological studies of ancient societies, Theissen offers a different reading. First, he notices that 'wise', 'powerful' and 'of noble birth' are all sociological terms, describing particular social groupings. Second, he notes the obvious yet often overlooked fact that 'not many' means 'some'. Indeed, these may be the people Paul explicitly mentions. Attention to those Corinthians named in the text, and how they are described, in terms of their social status has proved to be illuminating:

- Crispus (1 Corinthians 1.14) originally an *archisunagōgos* (literally 'ruler of the synagogue', Acts 18.8), a post usually entrusted to a wealthy man because it involved responsibility for care of the synagogue building (also Sosthenes, Acts 18.17 and 1 Corinthians 1.1).
- Erastus (Romans 16.23): there is uncertainty as to the precise meaning of *oikonomos tēs poleōs* (NRSV 'city treasurer'), though he can be assumed to be among the higher social strata (especially if this is the same Erastus who became aedile of the city and paid for a marble pavement to be constructed by the city's theatre).
- Reference to someone's 'house' is a probable guide to high social status (for example, 'the household of Stephanas', 1 Corinthians 1.16): the reference to 'those of the emperor's household' at Philippians 4.22 provides an example of a household that includes slaves, as also does Philemon 2. Gaius is host to Paul 'and to the whole church' (Romans 16.23), thus having a largish house in Corinth.

Theissen also highlights references to travel. This did not necessarily imply high social status (dependent workers, and even slaves, could travel). However, it at least suggests that some Corinthian Christians were merchants or in business (perhaps Chloe's people; possibly Phoebe, who delivers Paul's letter from Corinth to the Romans, Romans 16.1).

Theissen goes even further, suggesting why those baptized by Paul (1 Corinthians 1.14–17) were from the upper strata of society. Paul turned first, as a Hellenistic Jew might, to the Gentile 'Godfearers' (as well as the Jewish Crispus), who were eager to accept a form of Judaism that gave them full status as Gentiles, without becoming Jews. This provides a sociological explanation for Paul's conflict with other Jews: with its circumcision-free gospel, the Pauline mission was luring away the very Gentiles who were Judaism's patrons.

To do

How might issues of social stratification and socio-economic status shed light on the problem highlighted by Paul at 1 Corinthians 11.17–34? Try to identify the different social groupings implied by this passage, and their characteristics. Note also the light shed by archaeology on the probable size of Corinthian house-churches and the physical constraints under which they were likely to have operated (helpful here is Jerome Murphy-O'Connor, 2002, *St Paul's Corinth*, 3rd revised edition; Collegeville: Liturgical Press, pp. 178–85).

Patronage

What exactly was patronage, and how might it shed light on aspects of the New Testament? Patronage was a system of socially unequal but reciprocal relationships between a lower-status person with particular needs (a 'client') and a higher-status person capable of meeting those needs (a 'patron'). In the Roman world of the New Testament, the emperor was a kind of super-patron at the top of the pyramid, whose good favour was required for social advancement within the empire. Locally, powerful and wealthy Roman officials would have been patrons to local citizens (though they were 'clients' of the emperor and brokers who mediated with his lower-status clients on his behalf). But patronage was not restricted to officials: other people with influence could also provide patronage to those in need. Heads of households, for example, established patron–client relationships with freedmen, literary friends, philosophers and others in need of financial or other support.

John Chow has made an in-depth study of patronage as it would have impacted upon the social relationships of Christians in Corinth.[47] He lists the following seven characteristics of the relation between the patron and the client:

- *an exchange relationship*: the patron gives the client what the client needs (usually tangible: for example, land, a job, economic support); in return, the patron receives what he wants (for example, the publicizing of the patron's good name, voting in his favour);
- *an asymmetrical relationship*: only the patron has direct access to scarce resources;
- *a particularistic and informal relationship*: resources are not bestowed universally, but to the client: this particularistic aspect strengthens the relationship;
- *usually a supra-legal relationship*: based on mutual understanding between the patron and client;
- *often a binding and long-range relationship*: it carries with it a strong sense of interpersonal obligation;
- *a voluntary relationship*: at least in theory, though often not in practice;
- *a vertical relationship*: thus preventing solidarity developing between clients of the same patron; in times of crisis, a client would be expected to serve his leader and become a member of a faction.

Chow's analysis (building on the work of his predecessors) has made a good case for patron–client relationships being an important element in a number of issues that plagued the Corinthian church as revealed in 1 Corinthians. Given the 'upwardly mobile' nature of Roman Corinthian society, and the 'agonistic' nature of ancient society, there are likely to have been a good number of wealthy people in Corinth, in competition with each other for honour and the status of patron. Examples of how this might affect the Corinthian church include the following:

- *Paul's refusal of money*: the offer of money to Paul by wealthy and powerful Corinthians could be viewed as an attempt on their part to extend their patronage to Paul. His refusal would have been regarded as dishonouring them. From their perspective, he would not have looked like an apostle for his refusal of financial support.

- *Tensions at the Eucharist*: Theissen's analysis has already identified a likely socio-economic aspect to the disunity at the Corinthian Eucharist (1 Corinthians 11.17–34). However, patronage adds a further dimension to this scenario. It is not impossible that, rather than everyone bringing his or her own food to the Lord's Supper, it was all provided by wealthy patrons. Furthermore, if conventional practice in clubs or private feasts were followed, more and superior food would have been given to the patron and his or her social equals, thus accentuating the differences between patrons and clients. Social inferiority would have also been stressed by seating arrangements.

- *Maintaining Relationships with Pagans*: it is interesting that, underlying a number of 'problems' in 1 Corinthians, seems to be a desire on the part of some Corinthians to maintain their ties with pagans. In the case of the man living with 'his father's wife' (1 Corinthians 5.1: his stepmother?), the woman may well be a non-Christian, given that Paul only passes judgement on the man. At 1 Corinthians 6.1, we hear of at least one Corinthian Christian taking another to court before a pagan judge. There are also members of the church who apparently continue to frequent pagan temples (1 Corinthians 8.10; 10.1–22).

Again, theological explanations are often sought for this: they are 'spiritual' people influenced by Gnosticism, or Hellenistic enthusiasm, or Hellenistic-Jewish traditions. But social-scientific critics will ask about the *social context* within which such theological positions emerge. For Chow, it is possible that these people were among the powerful patrons of the church. They would have sought to maintain their links in order to continue to influence and be influenced by the life of the wider city. In turn, their clients would not have easily been able to challenge or criticize them for particular stances they might be taking.

> **Reflection**
>
> Think about the kinds of issues that might arise for Christians within a patron–client system (both for Christians who were patrons, and those who were clients). What particular scenarios might there be in a city like Corinth where one's patron–client obligations and one's Christian faith might come into conflict? How might Paul's analogy of 'the Body' in 1 Corinthians 12 speak to the patron–client system?

The Social Function of Ritual

Sociological insights have also contributed to our understanding of the function of early Christian ritual. Building on the insight of Durkheim that ritual not only conveys information but also does something, Wayne Meeks has explored the social function of two fundamental rituals of Pauline churches, baptism and the Eucharist.[48]

In Paul's terms, baptism signified a passing through death (Romans 6.3f.), a leaving behind of the old life (Romans 6.6f.), particularly important for those from a pagan background, such as in Corinth: 'But you were washed, you were sanctified, you were justified in the name of the Lord Jesus Christ and in the Spirit of our God' (1 Corinthians 6.11).

Similarly, the Eucharist or Lord's Supper is a ritual meal which defines a particular group over against other groups (including voluntary associations and trade guilds which had their own ritual meals), and denotes a break with former pagan lives: the 'cup of blessing that we bless' and the 'bread that we break' cannot be shared by those who participate in the 'table of demons' (1 Corinthians 10.16–21).

Meeks suggests that both baptism and the Eucharist have the social function of defining the boundaries of this new community. Some such social ritual would have been particularly important given that the Pauline Christians had abandoned the purity rules of Judaism, the very things which had enabled the Jewish communities to define their boundaries in a hostile world. Baptism, then, is not simply another 'rite of passage' to another stage of human development, but entry into another symbolic universe, from 'the realm of sin' to 'the realm of God', although the boundaries remained somewhat ambiguous (for example, Corinthians were not forbidden to eat with pagans – 1 Corinthians 10.27).

The Significance of Names

Finally, let us return to names. One of Theissen's contributions to the study of 1 Corinthians, as noted above, was to note the significance of named individuals (for example, Gaius, Erastus), and what might be gleaned from their description about their social status. This is highly illuminating, particularly given the way in which most readers of the New Testament skim across large numbers of personal names – Jason, Titius Justus, Ampliatus, Tryphosa, Syntyche, Crescens, Carpus, Demas, Persis, Alexander the coppersmith – without giving them a second glance. Indeed, it is not simply what is said about them, but their names themselves, that can tell us something (just as today we might take educated guesses about the place of origin of people called Juan Carlos or Stavros, Sinead or Olga, Paddy or Jock). Here are two ancient examples from the Pauline letters:

> I *Tertius*, the writer of this letter, greet you *in the Lord*. *Gaius*, who is *host* to me and *to the whole church*, greets you. *Erastus*, the *city treasurer*, and *our brother Quartus*, greet you. (Romans 16.22–3; italics mine)

- Gaius and Erastus have already been mentioned above. Both seem to be prominent figures: Gaius because he has a house large enough to accommodate 'the whole church'; Erastus because he is 'city treasurer' (although this might be an office that could be held by a slave or freedman).
- Both names (Gaius and Erastus) are Latin, which should not surprise us in first-century Corinth, which was a Roman colony (although Paul writes to and from Corinth in Greek, inscriptions found in the city reveal that Latin was used there, at least on public monuments).
- Similarly, both Tertius (whose occupation seems to be that of a profes-

sional scribe) and Quartus have Latin names. In most English translations, these names are transliterated. If we translated them, however, they
would be called Third and Fourth respectively (there is a Secundus or
'Second' mentioned at Acts 20.4). This suggests that they were slaves. If so,
they may have become Christians along with their masters.
- This points to the radical element in the Christian gospel: 'in the Lord',
the slaves Tertius and Quartus would not simply be persons designated by
their number, but 'brothers', kinsfolk of Paul and other Christians, with
all the obligations that entailed.

Greet *Prisca and Aquila*, and the *household of Onesiphorus. Erastus* remained in Corinth; *Trophimus* I left ill in Miletus. Do your best to come
before winter. *Eubulus* sends greetings to you, as do *Pudens and Linus
and Claudia* and all the brothers and sisters. (2 Timothy 4.19–21; italics
mine)

- Prisca (Priscilla) and Aquila are encountered on a number of occasions
(for example, Acts 18.2; Romans 16.3; 1 Corinthians 16.19), as a husband and wife team who first met Paul in Corinth, and made their way to
Ephesus (the implied destination of this letter), and then back to their old
home of Rome (if Romans 16 is addressed to that city). Their names are
Latin (*aquila* means 'eagle'; according to Acts 18.2, Aquila is a Jew from
Pontus in Asia Minor). The fact that Prisca is mentioned (unusually for a
woman) before her husband may suggest her pre-eminent status.
- Erastus the Corinthian makes an appearance here again. Trophimus is
mentioned at Acts 20.4 and 21.29: he was an Ephesian.
- Onesiphorus bears a Greek name, meaning 'profitable'. The fact that
he has a 'household' points to his relatively high social and economic
status. Eubulus is also a Greek name, translated as 'prudent' or 'of good
counsel'.
- The rest of the names here are Latin (Rome being the location of the implied author, 2 Timothy 1.17). Irenaeus (*Against Heresies* 3.3.3) identifies
this Linus with the Linus who was Bishop of Rome *c.*66–*c.*78. The last
name, balancing that of Prisca at the beginning of this section, is that of a
woman, Claudia.

To do

Read the list of greetings to those known to Paul at Romans 16.3–15. With the help of dictionaries, lexicons, commentaries and web searches, try to answer the following questions: Which have Latin names and which Greek? Which are male and which female? Do their names tell us any more about ethnic origin, or social status? Do their names mean anything? From what Paul says about them, which of them are Jewish? How many have 'houses', and what does this suggest? How many different groupings seem to make up the Roman church? (Note that there are some scholars, now a minority, who think Romans 16 was addressed to the church in Ephesus rather than in Rome.)

Further Reading

John Elliott, 1995, *Social-Scientific Criticism of the New Testament*, London: SPCK.

Philip Esler, 1994, *The First Christians in their Social Worlds*, London and New York: Routledge.

Bruce J. Malina, 1983, *The New Testament World: Insights from Cultural Anthropology*, London: SCM Press.

Wayne Meeks, 1983, *The First Urban Christians*, New Haven and London: Yale University Press.

Gerd Theissen, 1982, *The Social Setting of Pauline Christianity*, ET Edinburgh: T. & T. Clark.

9

Acknowledging One's Commitments

Where Do I Stand?

The city of Oxford where I live and teach evokes a range of images and emotions. For some it is a place of learning par excellence, which continues to leave its mark on the contemporary world in political, scientific and religious spheres. For others, it evokes a romantic and idyllic past, reinforced by the fine views of 'the dreaming spires' from places like Boar's Hill. From a different perspective, that past (and aspects of its present) is a world of decadence and social inequality which deserves to be unmasked and confronted.

But Oxford is in fact so much more than the world of its two universities (the University of Oxford and Oxford Brookes University). For many, it is the place of work and business, and a vibrant shopping centre for the county. It is the city of industry, typified by the Cowley car works. The vibrant, multiracial and multifaith East Oxford where my college is located offers another world, full of different voices, unknown to the many who fail to cross Magdalen Bridge from the city centre. The Oxford viewed through the eyes of the city's large number of homeless people looks very different from that seen by the casual day visitor, the student lodger in Jericho, or the wealthy house-owner of North Oxford. The one Oxford yields a range of very different 'Oxfords', not all of them visible to the same individual. Where I stand, and what my particular commitments are, dramatically affect my capacity to see, to hear and to perceive.

This is no less true when it comes to reading and interpreting the New Testament. A range of recent approaches have forced us to take seriously the extent to which our perspective, and the commitments we have, affect our ability to read. The New Testament story we read, the way we make sense of the world of the text, the questions we ask about it, the way we describe the centre and the margins, are affected by our location, our social and economic status, and the influences upon us.

To begin with, none of us starts reading from a neutral stance. Even the most careful ancient historian can never fully be disengaged from his or her own world, cultural norms and expectations. I can only begin to make sense of a text, or a world described in or lying behind that text, because I have an initial *pre-understanding*. This can be refined and challenged; but without some pre-understanding, I am unable to begin to understand. My life experience, education, the way in which those who have influenced me have interpreted, personal commitments I have to groups and institutions, all play their part. Consider the following verse from Paul's second letter to the Corinthians:

> Therefore, to keep me from being too elated, a thorn was given me in the flesh, a messenger of Satan to torment me, to keep me from being too elated. (2 Corinthians 12.7)

In the process of reading and making sense of the English words on the page (or the Greek words if I am capable of understanding Greek), I rely on existing understandings in order to understand what this particular juxtaposition of words might mean. Particular phrases might conjure up particular learned associations.

- Paul's 'thorn in the flesh', for example, has become legendary, even if there is widespread disagreement as to what this refers to. Am I predisposed to understand this 'thorn in the flesh' in a particular way, because of what I have been taught? Indeed, the fact that I regard the 'thorn in the flesh' as crucial to understanding this verse may be indicative of its importance in the interpretative community in which I stand.
- I might have an initial pre-understanding of what 'flesh' means here: do I understand the word negatively or positively? More significantly, am I predisposed to think of Paul using it negatively or positively?

- Another key phrase might be 'a messenger [or 'angel'] of Satan'. If I have been fed on a diet of late-night horror films, I will probably associate Satan with the sinister Prince of Darkness. Or I might have in mind the more primitive view of the Satan as a servant of God, 'the accuser', as in the book of Job.

Subsequent readings, greater familiarity with the rest of Paul's letters, or listening to and debating with other readers, might challenge me to refine or revise my initial understanding.

Thinking about Perspective

So, if none of us starts to interpret with a blank page, none of us reads from a neutral perspective. All readings are made from a committed stance, even if we are unaware of it or unwilling to admit it. Similarly, all texts are written from a particular stance. The readings explored in this chapter are explicit in this recognition, and seek to confront others with the stance from which they read. They ask questions like:

- What is the perspective from which the text is written? Are there hidden voices within or behind the text?
- What is the perspective of each individual reader, and how does that affect interpretation?
- What happens when divergent readings and perspectives come together?

While they often apply a 'hermeneutic of suspicion' to the text, and to particular interpreters, it is important to remember that acknowledgement of one's perspective is not unduly negative. One who reads the New Testament from a religious perspective, for example, is open to a dimension of the text shared with its authors. This profound dimension will be lacking to those who read the text with overtly atheistic presuppositions. On the other hand, one's Christian tradition – which includes prioritizing particular texts and reading them in a particular way – may blind one to other possibilities. Protestant Christians may be predisposed to read New Testament texts through the lens of Paul, and especially his teaching about justification. Roman

Catholic Christians may give more priority to the gospels, perhaps especially the Gospel of John. But even Roman Catholic and Protestant interpreters are far from monochrome. They will come from different cultures and language groupings; they will be married, widowed or divorced, single or celibate, male or female, parents, children or grandparents, heterosexual or gay.

How might one's perspective (or range of perspectives and commitments) affect the reading of the famous parable of the Prodigal Son (Luke 15.11–32)? Sermons are regularly preached on this complex story, which understand it rather differently depending on whether it is interpreted from the perspective of the younger son or of the father. Occasionally, the perspective of the elder son is considered as the interpretative key. This may indeed bring us close to the effect of the parable on the original audience, for first-century Jews would be predisposed to side with the son who has remained with his father, preserving the family inheritance. The shock value in the father's reaction to the wayward son would then call for a radical rethinking of values.

But there are other perspectives still, which may offer very different readings of this story. Those readers who are mothers might notice the complete absence of the mother from this story, and seek to supply that forgotten voice. Those committed to animal welfare might raise questions about the killing of a fatted calf to celebrate the younger son's return. There may be other moral criticisms to make: the world presupposed by this story is one in which slavery is the norm. How should this be read in a context in which Christians regard slavery as sinful and a form of oppression? The parable opens up a range of possibilities and questions, depending upon where one stands when reading it.

Reflection

Write down aspects of your own perspective that might impinge on your reading of the Bible: religious affiliation, culture, social background, gender, age, economic status, education, sexual orientation. How might these affect your reading of a particular New Testament passage? What positive contribution might they make? How might they limit your perspective, and make you 'blind' to aspects of a text?

Feminist Readings

One important perspective that has had a strong influence on New Testament scholarship is that of feminism. Feminist critics pay particular attention to gender in the New Testament texts, critiquing the androcentric ('male-centred') assumptions, and identifying the marginalization of women in them. More than that, however, they attempt to show how far androcentric views have determined the interpretation of these texts by subsequent commentators, so as to prevent the New Testament being experienced by women as liberating. Like other contemporary readings explored in this chapter, feminist critics apply a *hermeneutic of suspicion* to the text (reading 'against the grain' of the text), and to the work of interpreters. More positively, in 'reading for gender', they aim to recover forgotten voices (a classic attempt at this is Elisabeth Schüssler Fiorenza's *In Memory of Her*),[49] and to highlight positive feminine images and characters in the texts, sidelined or unseen by centuries of male interpreters.

Feminist readings are not so much an approach (they use a variety of interpretative approaches, historical, social-scientific, literary), as an ideological stance from which to interrogate the biblical text. First, they explore (and expose) the extent to which the New Testament books are written from an androcentric perspective, presupposing a patriarchal world-view. In the book of Revelation, for example, female characters on the whole are female stereotypes as they appear to males (virgin brides and seductive whores). The genealogy of Jesus in Matthew 1 focuses on the fathers, and his birth narrative on Joseph rather than Mary (compare Luke's, which has a more careful balance of male and female characters: Zechariah and Mary, Simeon and Anna). Even within Matthew's androcentric framework, however, there are hints of another possibility: the naming of the women in the genealogy, including Mary, opens up God's capacity to act in a radically new, non-patriarchal way in Christ.[50]

Second, feminist critics reveal the extent to which the contours of New Testament interpretation have been drawn up by men. For example, how many commentators ask questions about the daughter of the Syro-Phoenician woman when exegeting that gospel story? How often is the story of the Samaritan woman in John 4 interpreted negatively in terms of the woman's sexual past (what of her 'husbands'?)? How legitimate is the long-standing (though not universal) identification of the 'elect lady' of 2 John 1 not as a prominent woman within the Johannine communities but as a local church? Given the regular use of the Greek word *kuria* (and the Latin *domina*) to describe a *materfamilias*, and the parallel reference to Gaius at 3 John 1, an alternative reading might suggest itself. If textual transmission is an indication of later interpretation, then androcentric assumptions may creep in here too. In the Western text of Acts (Codex D), for example, Damaris, Paul's female convert in Athens, disappears from the text, while the male Aquila is mentioned *before* his wife Priscilla at Acts 18.26. In the case of English translations, feminist interpreters have fuelled the debates as to whether the Greek *adelphoi* in Paul's letters should be translated 'brethren', 'brothers' or 'brothers and sisters' (is he only addressing male Christians within his communities?).

Third, feminist interpretation attempts to reconstruct early Christian history as women's history. Elisabeth Schüssler Fiorenza's *In Memory of Her* is a case in point. She takes as her starting point the story of the woman who anoints Jesus. Despite Jesus' promise that 'what she has done will be told in remembrance of her' (Mark 14.9), not even the name of this woman has survived, in contrast to male disciples such as Peter and Judas. Yet the presence of the story – reworked in various forms in the gospels – hints at a half-remembered history of female disciples. Fiorenza attempts to listen to the silences, and piece together evidence for the activity and ministry of women within the early Church, despite the androcentric tendencies of the New Testament authors, redactors, copyists and interpreters. Stories like that of the Syro-Phoenician woman and the woman of Samaria come to the fore, as well as references to the Galilean women associated with Jesus' ministry and witnesses to the empty tomb. What forgotten roles within the early Christian movement might these narratives testify to? Fiorenza detects strong hints that Jesus' own ministry challenged patriarchal structures and world-views through its open table fellowship, its picture of a new 'family' of equal discipleship not based on blood ties, and critique of purity laws which especially impinged upon women.[51]

Similarly, Fiorenza pays attention to those neglected allusions to the status and role of often prominent and wealthy women within the Acts of the Apostles: for example, Mary the mother of John Mark, who has a 'house' in Jerusalem; Tabitha of Jaffa; Lydia of Thyatira who is Paul's first convert in Europe; Damaris in Athens. 'Yet', maintains Fiorenza, 'women's actual contribution to the early Christian missionary movement largely remains lost because of the scarcity and androcentric character of our sources.'[52]

Another example is Gail O'Day's illuminating feminist study of the Canaanite woman story in Matthew 15. In contrast to most readings of the story, O'Day attempts to show how it is the woman herself, not Jesus, who is the protagonist in the story.[53] She alone in the story initiates. Jesus first refuses to say anything. He then speaks, but only to his disciples. Only then, again at the woman's prompting, does Jesus speak: first to rebuff her with talk of 'dogs', finally to praise her faith in an apparent volte-face. In articulating that faith, she – a hated Canaanite – uses the language of Israel's psalms of lament, revealing her faith to be more authentically Jewish than many Jews who encountered Jesus. As O'Day puts it:

> Jesus was changed by this woman's boldness. Just as God is impinged upon by Israel's pleas, so is Jesus impinged upon here. The Canaanite woman knows who Jesus is and holds him to it; she will not settle for a diminishment of the promise. She insists that Jesus be Jesus, and through her insistence she frees him to be fully who he is.[54]

Revisiting the Story of Mary Magdalene

By way of another example, what might a feminist reading of John 20.1–18 look like? What kinds of questions might it ask? This passage contains John's distinctive version of the discovery of the empty tomb, and Mary Magdalene's encounter with the risen Lord in the garden cemetery. This memorable story has inspired countless artists to capture that moment when the risen Jesus, mistaken for the gardener, declares to Mary, 'Do not hold onto me' (the Latin translation *Noli me tangere* providing the traditional title for such artistic portrayals). But there are particular types of questions which a feminist interpreter might ask. Below are some suggestions, which you might like to explore (there may well be others which spring to mind):

- What has happened to the other women? In John's story, only Mary Magdalene is mentioned, whereas in the other gospels she comes to the tomb with other female companions ('the other Mary' in Matthew, Mary the mother of James and Salome in Mark, Joanna, Mary the mother of James and 'the other women' in Luke). Have the others been 'written out' in order to downplay the role of the women at this point? Or does their absence serve positively to highlight the prominent role of Mary? If so, what is that role?
- Why have the two male disciples (Peter and the beloved disciple) been introduced? The story of their discovery of the empty tomb (verses 2–10) effectively interrupts the flow of the narrative, in which Mary first discovers the tomb empty, and then encounters the risen Lord. Source critics would detect here the combination – not very smoothly executed – of two independent stories. Is this to bolster the apostolic authority of the empty tomb story, connected to the inadmissibility of female testimony in a Jewish court? If so, what role for women such as Mary Magdalene has been obscured?
- What is the relationship between Mary and Jesus? The geographical location ('the garden') is the classic locus of female–male intimacy, from Adam and Eve onwards.[55] Moreover, intertextual reading suggests strong echoes of the sexually charged Song of Solomon, where the female lover goes through the city and eventually down into the garden in search of 'him whom my soul loves' (Song of Solomon 3.1–5; 6.2–3). When she finds him, she holds onto him and will not let him go, anticipating the *Noli me tangere* moment of John's scene (Song of Solomon 3.4). Who, then, does Mary symbolize, as the Bride of the Bridegroom? How does she relate to female and male followers of Jesus (given the traditional equating of the Bride with the Church)?
- How far are established gender relations and roles challenged here, and how far are they simply reinforced? Does this narrative offer any surprises in the way in which the male Christ, or the female Mary, act and relate to one another?

- What role is accorded to Mary, as she is commanded to announce the Lord's resurrection and impending ascension to his 'brothers' (verses 17–18)? Has she been deprived of the full significance of her medieval title *apostola apostolorum* ('[female] apostle of the apostles') by centuries of androcentric interpretation? Or is her role essentially different from that of 'the disciples' (verse 18), unrelated to the subsequent apostolic preaching of the Church?

To do

Using a concordance, locate the references in Paul's letters to the following women: Prisca; Apphia; Phoebe; Nympha. What is said about each? What social status and roles do these descriptions suggest (you might wish to refer to commentaries on the relevant verses)? What kinds of questions might a feminist reader ask?

Other Liberationist Readings

Feminist criticism, concerned as it is for the liberation of women, can be seen as one specific example of a liberationist exegesis. Such readings represent a stance vis-à-vis the New Testament texts which seeks to read them as liberating, particularly for the marginalized (unmasking in the process that which fails to liberate). For feminists, the marginalized are women; for other liberationist readings, they may be particular racial groups, or gays, or the materially poor. Readings from the perspective of the latter are most obviously recognized as liberationist readings, influenced by liberation theology which first emerged in Latin America, but which has assumed new forms in other parts of the globe. An accessible introduction to liberationist readings is Christopher Rowland and Mark Corner's book, *Liberating Exegesis*.[56]

Liberationist readings, like the closely related feminist readings, ask the following types of questions: Whose interests are being served by particular interpretations of texts? Do interpreters have a vested interest (whether conscious or unconscious) in upholding particular positions? How might these texts be read as liberating for the poor? They are keen to draw attention to the socio-economic and political dimensions of the New Testament text, often hardly noticed by Western exegetes. A number of the parables of Jesus, for example, concern landowners, tenant farmers and hired labourers, reflecting the socio-political realities of first-century Galilee. The way in which such parables are understood by contemporary labourers who experience wealthy landowners as unjust and oppressive may be very different from established Western readings.

Their most obvious difference from the usual reading strategies espoused by the academy, however, is their starting point. They begin not with the context of the author, or the text, but the contemporary context of the poor, reading through the eyes of the poor. Typical of such grassroots reading is Carlos Mesters' paradigm for biblical interpretation, reflecting his own experience in Brazil:[57]

- *See* (one's present situation, which for many is the experience of oppression)
- *Judge* (understanding the reasons for this situation, relating it to the Bible's story of the liberation of God's people)
- *Act* (on the basic of the judgement made)

Mesters' paradigm attempts to articulate the pattern of interpretation used by basic Christian communities throughout Latin America. It does not necessarily pay attention to the historical context within which the New Testament writings were originally written (though trained experts inject historical-critical and other scholarly concerns into the dialogue as a check). Rather, it begins with the experience of the poor and oppressed, and their dialogue with the text in the light of their own situation. The communal nature of this exercise is important: it is no individualistic reading of the meaning of the text *for me*, nor confined to narrowly 'spiritual' or 'religious' concerns. Rather, it is a corporate dialogue, and one rooted in and speaking to the concrete circumstances of the poor and oppressed. A good example of this is *The Gospel in Solentiname*, a collection of reflections on the Sunday gospel readings emerging from a group of campesinos in Nicaragua and collected by Ernesto Cardenal.[58] These reflections are striking in their concern to address the concrete political and economic situation of the community.

Another example of Latin American liberationist exegesis is Elsa Tamez's insightful book on the letter of James, appropriately called *The Scandalous Message of James,* arising out of her Costa Rican situation.[59] James has often been sidelined in the West, not least among churches of the Reformation in the light of Luther's negative assessment. With its insistence that faith without works is dead (James 2.17), it seemed to sit uncomfortably alongside a Lutheran understanding of justification by faith. Within a Latin American context of dire poverty and injustice, however, James emerges as a highly subversive and provocative document, with a fierce denunciation of economic exploitation. As Tamez puts it:

> If the Letter of James were sent to the Christian communities of certain countries that suffer from violence and exploitation, it would very possibly be intercepted by government security agencies.[60]

Whereas a Western reading of James might typically focus on its disagreement with Paul, or its use of the Jesus tradition, Tamez's reading asks who are identified as the oppressed within it: principally the materially poor, including widows and orphans (James 1.27). She then asks about the kind of praxis advocated by the letter. When James talks about 'patience' or 'endurance', this is not to be understood (as so often in the West) as being of the passive and submissive kind. Rather, it is the active, militant perseverance also espoused by the book of Revelation.

To do

Read the parable of the rich man and Lazarus (Luke 16.19–31), bearing in mind your own social and economic location. Where do you locate yourself in the story? How do you hear it: as a parable of consolation, or of threat, or something different? If you are not challenged by the parable, ask yourself why not. What is the problem with the rich man? Does this problem look different depending upon where you locate yourself in the story? What does being poor entail for Lazarus in concrete terms? In the light of your reflection, how should you act?

Global Readings

Latin American liberation exegesis has had an influence on interpretative communities in other parts of the world. Each context – Asian, African, Native American, etc. – is unique, and this gives birth to a multiplicity of voices and reading strategies that complement and challenge the dominant Western readings. In Asia, for example, Christianity is a minority religion in close proximity with dominant faiths such as Buddhism and Hinduism, with their ancient scriptures.

In recent years there has been a growing awareness – still in its early days – of the diversity of these voices, and the necessity that they are heard and enabled to listen to one another. Listening to such global readings makes us aware of our cultural blind-spots, and opens us up to possibilities in and forgotten dimensions of the New Testament writings (which themselves emerged in a multicultural context). They expose us to the concerns of other interpretative communities, reminding us that interpreters in different contexts see the same things differently, or regard different elements of the text as significant. Global readings, in short, offer an invitation to us to expand our horizons.

An accessible collection of such readings is the *Global Bible Commentary,* under the general editorship of Daniel Patte, which brings together interpreters from every continent, as well from a range of religious backgrounds (Roman Catholic, Orthodox, Anglican, Protestant, Jewish), with a majority coming from the 'two-thirds world'.[61] Among the New Testament contributions, Alejandro Duarte offers a compelling reading of Matthew from the perspective of one whose close friends were killed under the military dictatorship in Argentina. For Duarte, the slaughter of the innocents (Matthew 2) provides an important interpretative lens through which to read the gospel. Hopes raised by the birth of a Messiah who would set people free are apparently immediately shattered by the resulting death of the innocents. For Duarte, the deaths of these children (and the deaths of his own loved ones in Argentina) cast doubt upon Jesus' mission and identity as Messiah. Only in the light of the whole gospel does another possibility emerge:

> But on the cross Jesus demonstrates his solidarity with the killed children. By renouncing the use of absolute power following a power-centred ideology (the use of 'legions of angels,' 26:53), Jesus deconstructs the

mechanisms of power that engender the killing of the innocents or the disappearance of the 'others' through their marginalization.[62]

For Duarte, in the light of his Argentinian context, the important questions to put to Matthew relate to power, and the use of power in relation to the poor and 'disappeared'.

Another example is Nigerian Catholic priest Justin Ukpong's challenging reading of Luke's Gospel, especially Luke's view of mission. Reading from the perspective of the evangelized rather than the evangelizer, Ukpong offers a rather different reading of the traditional 'gospel for the Gentiles'.[63] In its vision of bringing the light of the gospel to those in darkness, the relative treatment of Jewish and Gentile characters reflects a contrast 'between the Jews as the children of light, who should know better, and Gentiles who dwell in darkness, of whom not much is expected in the first place.'[64] Further, Luke is criticized for his failure directly to confront colonial oppression in his presentation of Roman authorities, despite the elements in his Gospel that point to liberation for the poor. Ukpong traces the influence of this on European missionaries in Africa, who understood their task as bringing Christ to where he was not before, and who failed to challenge colonial exploitation of the Nigerian people. He calls for contemporary missionary practice to learn from the inadequacies of the Lucan model, which are challenged by the Johannine logos theology, and by aspects of Luke's Gospel itself.

To do

Gather a group of fellow students to read Mark's account of the Gerasene demoniac (Mark 5.1–20). Ideally, the group should comprise people of different genders and ethnic/cultural backgrounds. In preparation, ask people to reflect on the story, in the light of their own particular context and concerns, and come with a list of issues/ questions. In the joint session, listen to the range of perspectives and contexts that emerge, and how the different voices challenge and expand your own understanding of the story. For a point of comparison, you might like to read Hisako Kinukawa's contextual commentary on this story in Daniel Patte et al. (eds), *Global Bible Commentary*, pp. 368–71.

Postcolonial Readings

Justin Ukpong's commentary on Luke draws attention to the close relation-ship between colonialism and biblical interpretation. The term 'postcolonial' emerged in the late twentieth century to describe a wide variety of readings from the non-Western world which critique the influence of colonialism, including its influence on biblical interpretation, and articulate suppressed voices of colonialism's victims. R. S. Sugirtharajah gives the following work-ing definition of postcolonialism: 'scrutinizing and exposing colonial domin-ation and power as these are embodied in biblical texts and in interpreta-tions, and as searching for alternative hermeneutics while thus overturning and dismantling colonial perspectives.'[65] There is a danger here that the in-digenous people can be viewed in a wholly positive light, or exclusively as 'the victim', while the colonizer is the villain. At its best, postcolonialism is aware of this simple binarism and attempts to move beyond it.[66]

Sugirtharajah identifies three areas where postcolonial criticism can offer a corrective to more established readings:[67]

- It reveals the *Europeanization of New Testament scholarship:* for example, Sugirtharajah draws attention to the relatively recent division of Acts according to Paul's three 'missionary journeys'. This schema was used ex-tensively to support and justify European-sponsored missionary tours by (mainly Protestant) missionary societies in the eighteenth and nineteenth centuries. These saw themselves as bringing the civilizing influence of Christian/European culture, and often worked closely with trading com-panies such as the East India Company. Paul (often viewed as a European!) was seen as the great exemplar of such home-sponsored missionary activ-ity.[68] Indeed, the problem was compounded by the perception of the Bible (especially in the Authorized Version) as a classic of the Western literary tradition, rather than essentially an Eastern book or collection of books.
- It challenges *racialization*, which is often subtly embedded in New Testa-ment scholarship.
- It confronts the tendency to *negate 'the other'*: it is particularly striking how far African and Asian presences within the New Testament text are

overlooked or denied. African and Asian interpreters attempt to redress the balance. The African scholar Joseph Enuwosa, for example, reminds us of the significant references to Africa and Africans in the New Testament (Libya, Egypt, Ethiopia, Alexandria; the Ethiopian eunuch, Simon of Cyrene, the 'Queen of the South'). He also traces possible African influences on the teaching of Jesus and the theology of the New Testament (exploring, for example, parallels with Egyptian religion).[69] Similarly, Asian scholars challenge the Western dismissal of any Asian (especially Buddhist) influences on the New Testament.

The Eurocentric portrait of early Christianity dominant in Western scholarship is, admittedly, helped by the shape of the New Testament canon. The canon is dominated by Paul (13 out of 27 books are attributed to him, while the majority of Acts deals with his conversion and ministry), who was active in the Roman Empire, mainly in Asia Minor (Turkey) and Europe. However, it is easy to overlook the fact that centres of New Testament Christianity (for example, Syrian Antioch, Jerusalem, Galilee, even those in Asia Minor itself, such as Ephesus) are in Asia rather than Europe, while North Africa is regularly mentioned, and early traditions trace the spread of the gospel eastwards from the Holy Land to Edessa, Persia and even India. Unusually from a Western perspective, Richard Bauckham's book on the letter of James makes a compelling case for this epistle being addressed to Jewish Christian communities in the Eastern as well as Western Diaspora.[70]

To do

Look at the maps of the New Testament world in a Bible atlas (some are listed in the introduction), or in a study Bible. If you have access to the internet, links to various web-based maps can be found at www.ntgateway.com/maps.htm. How do they envisage this world? What is its centre? Have any New Testament passages been ignored or downplayed? How might postcolonialism challenge you to redraw these maps?

Listening to the Challenge of Scripture

The various approaches explored in this chapter, in their different ways, present important challenges to the ways in which many of us have been accustomed to read the New Testament. Not least, they reveal the extent to which supposedly 'objective' readings coming from the academy are themselves ideologically driven, betraying unacknowledged commitments and power-relations. Nevertheless, such readings are not always content to critique other interpreters; at times, they challenge the New Testament text itself. For many Christian readers, such a stance vis-à-vis the New Testament raises niggling questions. Shouldn't a reader or interpreter submit himself or herself to the challenge of scripture, rather than vice versa?

It is important here to note that wrestling with the New Testament scriptures – as Jacob wrestled with the angel in Genesis 32 – may actually be a sign that we recognize their authority. They are not texts to be thrown away or ignored, but to be listened to and grappled with. Second, what many of these approaches are doing is deconstructing certain texts and certain readings by appealing to other (perhaps forgotten) canonical voices, and even other elements within the same texts. If the New Testament is better understood as a polyphonic choir (with the occasional discordant voice) rather than one singing in unison, then commitment to scripture requires us to take those different voices seriously.

Nevertheless, it is an important dimension of the history of New Testament interpretation that readers have approached these texts in order for their own lives and readings to be challenged. As Nicholas King SJ put it, writing out of a South African context:

> it seems to me that the Bible is not an object of clinical study so much as a live and dangerous force that can address us today and in this country, that can challenge us and disconcert us and set us free and wonderfully enhance our lives.[71]

Ironically, it is the type of readings described in this chapter which have often confronted Western academic readers with the New Testament's challenging, subversive message. The following chapter will take up this challenge, exploring the different ways in which readers have approached the books of the New Testament *theologically,* that is, as speaking about God and as allowing God to speak through them. This does not exclude the process of wrestling Jacob-like with the text. But it is a pattern of reading that remains open to the surprise of the New Testament, its ability to catch unawares, to unnerve and ultimately to transform human lives.

Further Reading

A. K. M. Adam, 1995, *What Is Postmodern Biblical Criticism?* Minneapolis: Fortress Press.

Elisabeth Schüssler Fiorenza, 1983, *In Memory of Her: A Feminist Reconstruction of Christian Origins*, London: SCM Press.

Daniel Patte, J. Severino Croatto, Nicole Wilkinson Duran, Teresa Okure and Archie Chi Chung Lee (eds), 2004, *The Global Bible Commentary*, Nashville: Abingdon Press.

Christopher Rowland and Mark Corner, 1989, *Liberating Exegesis: The Challenge of Liberation Theology to Biblical Studies,* Louisville, Kentucky: Westminster John Knox Press.

R. S. Sugirtharajah, 2003, *Postcolonial Reconfigurations: An Alternative Way of Reading the Bible and Doing Theology*, London: SCM Press.

10

The New Testament and the Question of God

God and the New Testament

In 2004 the American New Testament scholar Jerome Neyrey (whom we have already met as an exemplar of social-scientific readings) published a book entitled *Render to God*.[72] What makes this book so significant is hinted at by its subtitle: 'New Testament Understandings of the Divine'. Although Neyrey continues to employ social-scientific models in his exploration of the subject, he sees himself as addressing a surprising gap in New Testament scholarship: God. Neyrey traces the origins of this book to a lecture given by Nils Dahl in 1975, entitled 'The Neglected Factor in New Testament Study'. Surprising it may be, but the main subject matter of the New Testament writings – the God of Israel and Father of Jesus Christ – is rarely the central focus of (modern) works of New Testament scholarship. Put simply, God is the neglected factor in New Testament study in the academy.

This reluctance to speak about God may strike the student of the New Testament as puzzling indeed. It means that *theology* in its strictest sense – speaking about God – is not a central concern for professional scholars. One reason for this may be the simple fact that, for many New Testament writers, and indeed for Christian interpreters of the New Testament, God is a given, often presupposed in the background rather than consciously argued for. 'Foreground' subjects might include the disciples, or the Corinthian community, or the Spirit, or Jesus himself. Issues such as the relationship between the Church and the people of Israel, or the place of the sacraments, or attitudes towards slavery, may also be in the foreground, and hence are more in evidence in discussions of New Testament thought.

Yet this did not stop early commentators from pursuing theological concerns. There are two further reasons why God is not so overtly on the agenda of contemporary New Testament scholarship, both connected with the dominance of the historical paradigm. First, many New Testament scholars see their role as historians (or more recently, literary critics), at best laying the groundwork on which theologians proper can build. They are often reluctant to commit themselves to the theological enterprise. That is for others, 'the theologians'. Second, historical criticism essentially treats the New Testament writings from the perspective of their human authors, whether Matthew or James or Paul. It is a set of methods developed in order to explore the historical dimension of these writings as the products of human individuals in the first century CE. Given this, the one whom Christians believe to be the divine author is bracketed out from the discussion.

However, it would be untrue to say that scholarship has ignored the theological dimension of the New Testament entirely. Attempts at 'New Testament theology' (or 'theologies'), understood in significantly different ways by different practitioners, have remained on the scholarly agenda. Within the churches, theological readings of the New Testament have not been obliterated. This has included both the capacity of these writings and their interpreters to speak about God, and the believed capacity of God to speak through these writings. But there are various hints that the academy too – or at least certainly voices from within the academy – is becoming more open to theology as one aspect of its brief.

Reading Theologically

It is instructive to compare the questions and concerns of a modern New Testament commentary with those of patristic writers ('the Fathers' of the early Christian centuries). We will take as our test case the Prologue of John's Gospel (John 1.1–18), which most would accept is a passage rich in theological potential. This is a richly lyrical poem or hymn, which describes the emergence of the Word or Logos from God's side, his coming as light into the world, his rejection by his own, and the manifestation of his glory to those who did accept him.

Standard modern commentaries on John, even on this most theological of passages, tend to begin with historical and literary questions. Noting the poetic style of the Johannine Prologue, they may ask questions about its literary form and its prehistory, perhaps as a hymn sung by the Johannine community. They may attempt to reconstruct the original form of this hymn, and hypothesize about its relationship to different editions of the gospel. In reflecting on the Christological title of 'the Word', they will probably focus on its Jewish parallels and antecedents, whether Genesis 1, Proverbs 8, or Philo's Logos speculation. More theological issues may then come into view, with the need to explore key terms such as life, light, 'the world', and how these relate to the Word/Logos. There may well be some theological reflection on how the Logos relates to God, and a discussion of how the various sections of the Prologue correlate with the history of salvation (for example, creation, the call of Israel and giving of the Law, the incarnation of the Word). However, even here focus will be on the theology of the original evangelist (or in literary terms, the narrator's 'point of view'), rather than the beliefs of the contemporary readership and the meaning of this Prologue for them.

Given these interests, reading a patristic commentary or homily on the same passage can be surprising, though also illuminating. A good example is provided by St Augustine's tractates or lectures on John's Gospel, delivered during the liturgy during his years as Bishop of Hippo Regius in North Africa. Augustine launches straight into overtly theological concerns, ignoring questions to do with literary antecedents and structure, and focusing on the text in its final form. He deals with such matters as the relationship between the Logos and the Father (confronting head-on Arianism and other heresies of the day), or the nature of that Logos/Word as opposed to transitory human words, or the meaning of that obscure phrase 'and grace for grace' (*et gratiam pro gratia*, John 1.16). In doing so, he is not afraid to cite other passages of scripture to clarify an ambiguity. This contrasts with more modern historical-critical commentators, who may refer to Old Testament passages in order to explore the origins of a concept like Logos, but who on the whole will regard each New Testament writer as self-contained. For

Augustine, given his patristic conviction that scripture is a coherent whole, there is nothing shocking in bringing in a passage from Romans or 1 Corinthians in order to make sense of an obscurity in John.

Augustine's ultimate concern, however, is not theological speculation, but how the theology impinges on the lives of his congregation. He wants them to get their understanding about the Word correct, in order that they might 'be new-made by the Word'.[73] For him, the meaning of John's Gospel *for us* is not an 'added extra' to the meaning of the text *in itself*. A theological reading – in the sense of clarifying what God has done for him and his congregation – is paramount in his understanding of biblical interpretation.

Of course, Augustine's tractates are sermons rather than strict commentary. One would expect a concern in a homiletic context for the theological meaning of the text for the congregation being addressed. Nevertheless, this prioritizing of theological interests is reflected in other patristic authors also. Origen's famous commentary on John's Gospel also offers a profoundly theological reading of the book. Origen is concerned with questions such as what is meant by the Logos being 'in the/a beginning', what is being said of the Son of God when he is called the Word, and the way in which Christ as the true light illuminates in a manner different from the created lights of sun, moon and stars.[74]

In short, if scripture is 'the word of God in human language' (a description used, for example, by the Roman Catholic Church's Pontifical Biblical Commission),[75] historical-critical methods tend to focus on the second part of this definition. Patristic exegesis in contrast, while not ignoring the second, places priority on the first. These are divine words, to enliven God's people, albeit mediated through the human words of their human authors.

Rediscovering Patristic Exegesis

There are signs within New Testament scholarship of a renewed interest in such patristic methods of exegesis. This interest is in fact one example of a growing recognition among scholars that New Testament interpretations of earlier (pre-Enlightenment) commentators have been too readily and unfairly dismissed. As an illustration, look at the bibliography in a recent scholarly book on the New Testament, and count up the number of books published before 1800, or even 1900. The impression one receives is that very little, if any, useful biblical interpretation was done before the end of the eighteenth century.

Indeed, the terminology used to describe it is instructive: 'pre-modern' or 'pre-critical', ignoring the extent to which patristic and medieval commentators noted variant readings, explored apparent conflict between New Testament authors, and debated questions of authorship. Origen's *Hexapla* is a good illustration of the critical nature of patristic scholarship: six versions of the Old Testament are set out side by side, complete with critical comments and discussion of variant readings.

C. H. Dodd's famous book on *The Parables of the Kingdom*, for example, famously begins with an extreme allegorizing version of the parable of the Good Samaritan (a simplified version of Augustine's reading), in order to show the deficiencies of patristic exegesis:

> *A certain man went down from Jerusalem to Jericho:* Adam himself is meant; *Jerusalem* is the heavenly city of peace, from whose blessedness Adam fell; *Jericho* means the moon, and signifies our mortality, because it is born, waxes, wanes, and dies. *Thieves* are the devil and his angels. *Who stripped him,* namely, of his immortality; *and beat him,* by persuading him to sin; *and left him half-dead,* because in so far as man can understand and know God, he lives; but in so far as he is wasted and oppressed by sin, he is dead; he is therefore called *half-dead.* The *priest* and *Levite* who saw him and passed by, signify the priesthood and ministry of the Old Testament, which could profit nothing for salvation. *Samaritan* means Guardian, and therefore the Lord himself is signified by this name. The *binding of the wounds* is the restraint of sin. *Oil* is the comfort of good hope; *wine* the exhortation to work with fervent spirit. The *beast* is the flesh in which He deigned to come to us. The being *set upon the beast* is the incarnation of Christ. The *inn* is the Church, where travellers are refreshed on their return from pilgrimage to their heavenly country. The *morrow* is after the resurrection of the Lord. The *two pence* are either the two precepts of love, or the promise of this life and of that which is to come. The *innkeeper* is the Apostle (Paul) . . .[76]

Few would deny that Augustine's reading takes the allegorizing process to an extreme. But many now feel that such passages give an unbalanced view of the diversity and richness of 'pre-modern' New Testament interpretation, and that even allegorical readings are not to be dismissed out of hand. Useful introductions to biblical interpretation in the early Church (of both Old and New Testaments) include the following:

- Karlfried Froelich (ed.), 1984, *Biblical Interpretation in the Early Church*, Sources of Early Christian Thought; Philadelphia: Fortress Press (includes examples of patristic exegesis).
- James L. Kugel and Rowan A. Greer, 1986, *Early Biblical Interpretation*, Philadelphia: Westminster Press (includes both Jewish and early Christian interpretation).
- John J. O'Keefe and R. R. Reno, 2005, *Sanctified Vision: An Introduction to Early Christian Interpretation of the Bible*, Baltimore and London: Johns Hopkins University Press.
- Manlio Simonetti, 1994, *Biblical Interpretation in the Early Church: An Historical Introduction to Patristic Exegesis*, ET Edinburgh: T. & T. Clark.

Reflection

What do you understand by the terms 'pre-modern', 'modern' and 'postmodern'? Or by the terms 'pre-critical' and 'critical'? What might the terms 'pre-modern' and 'pre-critical' imply about New Testament interpretation prior to *c.*1800? Revisit your reflections later, after you have looked at some examples of earlier interpretation and commentary.

Rejoining a Long Conversation

Luke Timothy Johnson, in an important and provocative book co-authored with William Kurz SJ, talks about the need for New Testament scholars (he has Roman Catholic scholars particularly in mind) to 'rejoin a long conversation'. By this he means rediscovering the rich diversity of earlier biblical interpretation, and re-engaging with forgotten but valuable aspects of such 'pre-modern' readings.[77] Not least, argues Johnson, this includes rediscovering the concern of earlier exegetes for growth in holiness and ecclesial engagement. He reminds us of that medieval adage that one reads the scriptures in order to gain wisdom (*sapientia*) and not simply knowledge (*scientia*).

Johnson has chosen his words carefully: what he advocates is a 'conversation', in which both sides contribute to the debate. He is not arguing for an uncritical return to an earlier age, nor is he unaware of the real benefits and advances achieved by post-Enlightenment critical scholarship. But he is critical of the either/or presuppositions of such scholarship, which has effectively silenced the centuries-old voices of Christian forebears.

Similarly, in a provocative article on patristic exegesis, Brian Daley sketches out several features of how the Fathers read scripture (both Old and New Testaments), from which contemporary Christian readers might profitably learn.[78] The following are some of the positive features of 'pre-modern' interpretation identified by Daley and Johnson:

- Its conviction of the reality of God, as the ultimate author of the New Testament texts, speaking in and through their distinctive voices.
- Its belief in the essential unity of the biblical narrative, and its conviction that, despite different perspectives and nuances, different parts of scripture speak harmoniously (without ignoring difficulties in the text, the patristic instinct is to find a way to resolve such difficulties positively).
- Its capacity to view the biblical text as diverse and open to a range of meanings, speaking at many levels: refusing to reduce the meaning of a passage to authorial intention, but allowing for the activity of the Spirit in the contemporary reader.
- Its integration of biblical study, theology, prayer and Christian life: the most famous exemplars of pre-modern scholarship being pastors, preachers and people of prayer.
- Its ability to imagine the world that scripture imagines (a wide world rather than a narrow world).
- Its concern for questions of truth: asking of any text, is it true, and if so, in what way?
- Its attention to the Rule of Faith (the outline of the basic Christian message,

as became formulated, for example, in the creeds), as providing the broad lens through which to read and interpret the text.

- Its conviction that the meaning of scripture involves the contemporary Christian reader: the quest is not so much for a passage's historical *Sitz im Leben* (as for the form critics), as its *Sitz in unserem Leben*, its setting in *our* life.
- Its conviction that biblical interpretation is to be undertaken within the community of the Church, aimed at building that Church up in love.
- Its application of a 'hermeneutic of piety' (Daley) or a 'hermeneutics of generosity or charity' (Johnson) rather than a 'hermeneutic of suspicion', approaching the text humbly and reverently, with prayer and fasting.

This rediscovery of patristic patterns of exegesis is reflected in several new commentary series which provide excerpts of patristic commentary on particular biblical books in English translation, or grapple with wider theological readings:

- *Ancient Christian Commentary* (general editor: Thomas C. Oden).
- *The Church's Bible* (general editor: Robert Louis Wilken).
- *SCM Theological Commentary* (general editor: R. R. Reno).

A number of patristic commentaries are also available in English on the world wide web:

- www.monachos.net/patristics/index.shtml.
- www.ccel.org/fathers2.
- www.newadvent.org/fathers.

To do

Select a commentary or homily by a patristic writer (or group of patristic writers) on a particular New Testament passage. Note the kind of questions the commentator is interested in. What aspects of this commentary are helpful, and what inappropriate to contemporary readers? Now compare the interests and questions of a modern commentary on the same passage.

Reading in a Tradition

Beside the Roman Catholic voices of Johnson, Kurz and Daley, members of other churches are advocating a similar rediscovery of the value of reading within a particular ecclesial tradition (see especially the ecumenical volume edited by Ellen F. Davis and Richard B. Hays, *The Art of Reading Scripture*, which contains Daley's article). Given that the New Testament arises out of the Christian community, and has a long history of interpretation within diverse Christian communities, is it not best read and interpreted within those ecclesial communities? Granted the distinctly religious message of the New Testament writings, should not would-be theologians and trainee clergy challenge what Mark Allen Powell calls the process of 'desensitizing' to 'personal reference' ('what the text means for us'), which dominates biblical scholarship?[79]

In response to such a call, New Testament scholars outside the churches may be concerned at this renewed interest in ecclesially based approaches which regard older ways of reading more positively. There is, for example, the real danger of scholarship losing its critical edge by blurring the historical gulf between the world of the ancient texts and that of the contemporary reader, or its academic freedom due to constraints placed on it by a particular Christian tradition. Others may wonder about the constraints on allegorical or figurative readings of the New Testament: can the text be made to mean anything? Further, many are concerned that emphasizing the essential unity of scripture may lead to a playing down or glossing over of the different voices within the New Testament canon, including those discordant voices. Finally, undue stress on a tradition's role in interpreting scripture plays down the ways in which that tradition needs at times to be challenged by scripture.

Such concerns need to be taken seriously. Nevertheless, the following points can be made in support of reading the New Testament from within and for a particular Christian tradition:

- It has a particular concern for a reading of the New Testament that will nourish the Christian community. What is not being denied is that there are other ways of reading the New Testament profitably (as a historical source, for example, or as inspirational literature), or that non-Christians, or Christians of other traditions, have perspectives to contribute from which others need to learn.

- It is based on the recognition that the New Testament writings are religious, theological documents, arising out of a community of faith. While there is a huge historical gulf between contemporary Christians and the first Christians, the two possess a fundamental shared conviction and experience, which enables a sympathetic entering into the religious message of the text.

- It acknowledges that the present generation does not have a monopoly on wise readings, but can profitably learn from interpreters of the previous 19 centuries (indeed, it is a reminder of the extent to which, often unconsciously, our readings are indebted to our predecessors).

- It challenges the view that a 'non-dogmatic' starting point is more academically liberating than reading within and for a particular tradition (for example, the anti-supernatural presuppositions of post-Enlightenment 'objective' scholarship). Indeed, some Christian scholars wonder how free scholarship in the academy often is, with its pressure to publish works that will not undermine 'academic credibility' and threaten tenure. Luke Johnson reminds his fellow Catholic scholars of the valued Catholic tradition of 'loyal dissent', which is able to push the boundaries from within rather than attacking antagonistically from without. Nor does standing confidently in a tradition rule out dialoguing with and being challenged by voices from beyond that tradition.

New Testament Authors as Theologians

Even within a historical paradigm, however, theological concerns need not be marginalized. As we saw in Chapter 6, redaction criticism of the gospels paid particular attention to the distinctive message of individual evangelists, including their theological emphases. To take one example, Matthew's account of the stilling of the storm (which is paralleled in Mark and Luke for

useful comparison) highlights particular aspects of Christ and his relationship to the disciples/Christian community:

> And when he got into the boat, his disciples followed him. A gale arose on
> the lake, so great that the boat was being swamped by the waves; but he
> was asleep. And they went and woke him up, saying, 'Lord, save us! We are
> perishing!' And he said to them, 'Why are you afraid, you of little faith?'
> Then he got up and rebuked the winds and the sea; and there was a dead
> calm. They were amazed, saying, 'What sort of man is this, that even the
> winds and the sea obey him?' (Matthew 8.23–7).

- The context in Matthew is slightly different, given the dialogue between
  Jesus and two would-be disciples about following him (verses 19–22),
  which now interrupts the beginning of the boat story (which strictly
  begins in verse 18: 'he gave orders to go over to the other side'). This has
  the effect of turning the boat into an allegory of the Church, into which
  disciples are to follow Jesus.
- Jesus is addressed with the words 'Lord, save us!' (acknowledging his
  lordship, and reflecting a liturgical prayer used by the post-Easter community). For Matthew, there is no sharp disjunction between the way in
  which Jesus acted during his earthly ministry and how the risen Lord now
  acts on behalf of the Church at prayer: the two are one and the same.
- His rebuking of the winds and sea (as in Mark and Luke) makes the story
  a theophany (a manifestation of God, who alone has control over the elements). The nature of Jesus' divine sonship is therefore raised in acute
  terms. Christ does no less than what God does.

Nor is the theological dimension restricted to the gospels. Paul himself
is often described as a 'pastoral theologian', in the sense that in his extant
letters he thinks theologically about the situations of his own fledgling
Christian communities. His conviction that the Corinthian church is one
body in Christ, with its implications for a host of 'mundane' issues (treatment of the poor; daily diet; behaviour at the Eucharist), is profoundly theological. So too his advice about marriage and celibacy in 1 Corinthians 7 is
framed within his thinking about the End-time breaking into the present.

The author of Acts arguably presents a theology of history, in which he grapples with the profoundly theological question of the justice and fidelity of God. The book of Revelation explores, in visionary form, the nature of a God who is encountered as both darkness and light, whose coming is experienced as both salvation and judgement.

Similarly, narrative approaches are often open to a theological dimension. Both the gospels and Paul (see Katherine Grieb's book on Romans referred to in n. 33) can be approached as attempts at doing theology through narrative. The evangelists, for example, explore the significance of Jesus of Nazareth through the story they tell about him.

Nevertheless, there are complicating factors. None of the New Testament writers are setting out to write 'a theology' (perhaps the nearest that come to it are Ephesians and Romans, though the latter is certainly responding to a specific context in Paul's own ministry and the life of Roman Christianity). Rather, they write in order to answer questions, engage in disputes, and proclaim the Christian gospel. They certainly have a theological vision, though that is so often under the surface, taken as read rather than articulated explicitly. Second, in reflecting on the theological dimension of these texts and their historical authors, should we simply be attempting to describe, for example, Paul's theological vision, or to grapple with it in the light of our own theological convictions and concerns, or indeed to learn more from the various moves he makes than from the specific answers he gives? Third, there are some strong voices urging that to see the New Testament writers primarily as theologians may in some cases be misguided. John Ashton's illuminating study of Paul, for example, argues that the apostle is better understood through the category of 'religion' than 'theology': a mystic, visionary and prophet rather than a systematic thinker.[80]

The Debate about New Testament Theology

Similar questions are reflected in the ongoing debate about that branch of New Testament scholarship know variously as 'New Testament Theology' or the 'theology of the New Testament' (and the related genre of scholarly books of the same titles). This enterprise has been envisaged in a number of different ways (a recent collection exploring its scope and possibilities is the Festschrift for Robert Morgan, himself an important voice in the discipline, edited by Christopher Rowland and Christopher Tuckett):[81]

- An attempt to produce a unitary 'theology of the New Testament', or a systematic presentation of its 'doctrinal concepts': which is inevitably selective, and involves the omission or suppression of some of the voices.
- A description of the individual 'theologies' of New Testament writers: although, as we have noted, the whole of an author's thought is rarely explicit in the text, rather than implicit in the background (for example, Jude is only 25 verses). This has the advantage of allowing different voices within scripture to contribute (though not all features of the texts may be 'doctrine', nor all of equal importance). It is, however, also inevitably abstract: drawing out from a New Testament book 'the theology of' that book or author is a different process from reading that book theologically.[82]
- An attempt to write 'the history of early Christian religion and theology' (Wrede),[83] with individual writers being included only when they have been particularly outstanding or epoch-making.[84] That is, historical reconstruction rather than theology proper, which does not restrict itself to the canonical writings.
- Engagement in a conversation, a dialogue with the New Testament texts, taking note of the ongoing theological tradition of the Church, and one's own ecclesial context, experience and concerns, so as to be able to 'speak about God today'.

To do

Choose a 'Theology of the New Testament' from your own or a library shelf (for example, Bultmann, Kümmel, Caird, Johnson, Esler). Skim through or look at the contents page, and ask yourself what the author is attempting to do. What are the pros and cons of this approach. Choose a section to read in more detail: in what ways does it help you understand the New Testament theologically? How might you approach it differently?

Encountering God: Lectio Divina

But theology is not only conceived in terms of speaking about God. There is a dimension of theology that has traditionally involved listening to God, allowing God to speak through the written word of scripture. The practice of *lectio divina* is a very ancient Christian way of praying and reading the scriptures, especially in the Western monastic tradition, loosely translated 'sacred reading' or 'reading in a godly manner'.[85] If contemporary New Testament scholars debate the relationship between original human author, written text and contemporary reader, *lectio divina* is concerned with that between the New Testament text, reader/pray-er and divine author. It has a traditional fourfold pattern (classically set out by the twelfth-century Carthusian Guigo II, prior of the Grande Chartreuse, in his *Ladder of Monks*):

- *lectio*: reading the text, bringing the words into the mind and heart; this was originally done aloud (which may be a better way to do it than our more common silent reading);
- *meditatio*: meditating, through repeating the words and mulling them over, allowing particular words or phrases to speak, and be digested; 'it [meditatio] is receiving and taking to heart a word that I believe is personally addressed to me';[86]
- *oratio*: prayer in response to the word which has spoken to us;
- *contemplatio*: contemplation or adoration, movement from the words of prayer to simply staying in God's presence ('wondering').

Perhaps the popularity of *lectio* within a monastic context is unsurprising, given its slow, reflective nature. But it has never been reserved to the monastic class. John Chrysostom had some rather harsh words for Christians who thought that prayerful reading of the scriptures is best left to the clergy, and especially the monks:

Some of you may say, 'I am not a monk . . .' But here you are mistaken, because you think that the Scriptures are meant only for monks, whereas they are actually far more necessary for you, the faithful who live in the midst of the world. The only thing more gravely sinful than not reading the Scriptures is believing that reading them is useless and serves no purpose.[87]

First, then, *lectio* requires a slowing down that many in our culture find difficult. Rather than rushing, or even attempting to read a whole New Testament book in its entirety, it invites us to read in a different gear, staying with a passage and chewing it over, so as to listen to what it might have to say to us. In the words of Michel de Verteuil, 'In lectio divina, we love the text, linger over it, read it over and over, let it remain with us.'[88]

Second, it presupposes that God speaks through the New Testament writings. Unlike a number of approaches described in this studyguide, it requires religious commitment. In order for this 'divine conversation' to happen, however, the right context for reading is required: a regular time, for example; a place where one can read slowly and prayerfully; an atmosphere of prayer and recollection.

Third, it is essentially a corporate act of reading, even when it is undertaken not in church with a body of monks but individually. It is a pattern of reading done within the life and faith of the Christian community, within a particular tradition, and drawing on the resources of that tradition to aid understanding. Indeed, many find it helpful to follow a Church lectionary in order to provide some pattern to *lectio divina*, and avoid simply focusing upon favourite passages.

Finally, *lectio* does not end with reading and prayer; it should lead to action in our own life, to 'doing the word' which has just been heard and reflected upon. This traditionally involves a threefold process:

- *discretio* or 'discernment' of the activity of the Spirit in my life;
- *deliberatio*, making a decision about God's will for me;
- *actio*, putting that into action.[89]

Lectio divina is a reading of scripture that cannot be learned except in the practice. Although there are books (for example, those of Michel de Verteuil already mentioned) that can provide us with examples, they are no substitute for the practice itself, for each person will hear and respond differently to the same passage (indeed the same person will respond differently at different times). Nevertheless, de Verteuil makes some helpful observations about *lectio*, in relation to those sections of the synoptic gospels that contain short pithy, loosely connected sayings of Jesus. In reflecting on Luke 12.35–40 ('Be dressed for action and have your lamps lit . . .'), he notes the following:

- we need to remember all the more with such passages to read very slowly, mulling each one over separately, since people tend to read such short sayings quickly;
- the sayings of Jesus are generally metaphorical, speaking to our imagination (rather than the more abstract thinking we are used to);
- they are also 'universally true': speaking not only of our relationship with God, but also our church communities, families, workplace, town, nation, world.

To do

Choose a passage from the gospels, and attempt to read it slowly, meditatively and with openness, according to the principles of *lectio divina*.

Further Reading

Ellen F. Davis and Richard B. Hays (eds), 2003, *The Art of Reading Scripture*, Grand Rapids, Michigan/Cambridge: Eerdmans.

Luke Timothy Johnson and William Kurz, SJ, 2002, *The Future of Catholic Biblical Scholarship*, Grand Rapids, Michigan/Cambridge: Eerdmans.

Christopher Rowland and Christopher Tuckett (eds), 2006, *The Nature of New Testament Theology*, Oxford: Blackwell.

11

The Ongoing Story

Who are the New Testament's Insightful Interpreters?

The discussion of patristic interpretation in the previous chapter hinted at a question which has become increasingly important in New Testament scholarship over the past decade or so: is insight into the meaning of the New Testament writings only, or primarily, to be found in the work of 'critical' scholars of the last 200 years or so? Did *real* understanding of the New Testament texts only begin with the Enlightenment? Or is there wisdom to be found in the previous 17 centuries of reading the New Testament?

Moreover, is insight most appropriately sought in the scholarly commentaries of whatever century? Or should we be looking in other directions, to sermons and marginal notes, to the diaries of visionaries and the meditations of contemplatives? Do we gain most from 'reading' human lives, such as that of Francis of Assisi, driven by a passion for the gospel and the Christ it proclaims?[90] Should we pay attention to how Christians pray, to hymns and prayers and antiphons, to the pattern of the Eucharist in memory of what Christ did, to the drama of the Orthodox Liturgy, so evocative of the angelic liturgy described in the book of Revelation? Or are the artists, poets and musicians among the more insightful of commentators? Scholarship is increasingly remembering that, for much of Christianity's history, Christians have been exposed to the story of Jesus and the early Church primarily through what they saw, and what they heard.

In other words, although the historical paradigm often envisages a 'dirty great ditch' (Lessing's *der garstige breite Graben*) separating the first-century New Testament texts and their human authors from the contemporary reader, there is in fact an unbroken – though incredibly diverse – chain of historical interpretation between the first and twenty-first centuries. People have read the New Testament in the fifth and the fifteenth centuries, and to varying degrees we stand on the shoulders, and are influenced by the readings, of those who have gone before us. Some suggest that we should rethink the image of the 'ugly ditch', envisaging instead 'a highly diverse landscape with a lot of ups and downs, unexpected views, side-valleys, plains and viewpoints and with a wealth of wonderful and sometimes very strange flowers.'[91]

Reception History of the New Testament

One major development in recent New Testament scholarship has been a growing interest in the reception history of the biblical books. Reception history is more than simply the 'history of interpretation', which is largely confined to describing how scholarly commentators have interpreted particular texts. Rather, it regards a host of other media – hymns, homilies, paintings, meditations, political tracts – as significant for gaining insight into the New Testament writings. As its name suggests, reception history is interested in how the New Testament books have been received over the centuries, on a fairly broad canvas.

Closely related to it (indeed, the two are often regarded as synonymous) is *Wirkungsgeschichte*, a German term coined by Hans-Georg Gadamer and variously translated 'effective history', 'history of effects' and 'history of influence'. If reception history explores the New Testament from the perspective of the recipients (how people at different times have received, responded to, the texts), *Wirkungsgeschichte* focuses on the texts themselves, and the effects (negative as well as positive) they have achieved. Ulrich Luz, however, whose work on Matthew's Gospel (notably his commentary in the ecumenical *Evangelische-Katholische Kommentar* series) pioneered *Wirkungsgeschichte* in New Testament scholarship,[92] argues that 'effective history' is a better translation of the term. This means that the contemporary interpreter is herself being carried on the stream of history, belongs to it, and cannot therefore examine it in a detached manner. The two come together in that studying reception history of New Testament books helps us to rediscover where we have come from (consciousness of 'effective history' or *Wirkungs-geschichte*).[93] Studying reception history and 'effective history' is valuable for the following reasons:

- It makes us aware of 'our' tradition (and that all of us have, and read in, a tradition, even if we have been used to thinking otherwise).
- It helps us to see more clearly where we stand, both the limits to our own perspective and the routes by which our interpretations have come about (including those to whom we are indebted, the 'giants' on whose shoulders we stand, and who have shaped the questions we put to the text).
- It broadens our own horizons by exposing us to readings beyond our own culture or tradition (an important contribution to the ecumenical move-ment among Christians). This means that reception history and *Wirkungs-geschichte* are no straightforward return to 'reading as the Church tells us' (though they include such forgotten ways of reading); they also ex-plore voices formerly considered as 'dissenting voices', and even those of non-Christians.
- In doing so, it points (as other 'pre-modern' and 'postmodern' approaches have already suggested) to the multivalency of the text: its capacity to speak at different levels, rather than possessing one fixed meaning. It points to the ambiguity of texts, and gaps in the text, which are interpreted or developed in different ways by interpreters.
- It also makes us aware of the extent to which historical and political events and social contexts have affected readings of the text, and what different people have seen as important within the same texts.
- It forces us to take seriously the negative 'effects' of New Testament texts as well as the positive: for example, it urges us to confront the shameful anti-Semitic effects of the gospel passion narratives, as well as their capacity to speak powerfully to those experiencing suffering and persecution.[94]
- It takes seriously the range of contexts and media within which the New Testament has influenced and been used by others in different historical periods. These include more popular perspectives not normally found in 'scholarly' works.

- It reminds us that attention to and comment on the minute details of a text (the characteristic of commentaries) is not the only way to appreciate and understand a text: a more impressionistic, or broad-sweep interpretation (perhaps that of an artist or mystic) may give a deeper insight into a book like Revelation, and its evocative and dramatic power, than a commentary that attempts to explain every verse.
- It challenges the distinction often made by critical scholars between the meaning of a text and its meaning *for us*.
- It is interdisciplinary, in that it forces New Testament scholars out of their narrow enclaves into conversations with historians, artists, art historians, musicians, poets and literary theorists.

Besides Luz's work on *Wirkungsgeschichte,* English-speaking readers might like to explore volumes in the Blackwell Bible Commentary series (BBC; explicitly a reception history series), under the general editorship of John Sawyer, Christopher Rowland and Judith Kovacs. Further information about this series can be found at its website: www.bbibcomm.net. The Oxford-based Centre for the Reception History of the Bible is engaged in interdisciplinary study of the biblical text, both Old and New Testament (www.crhb.org).

Some New Testament Examples

As an illustration of the contribution of reception history, let us look at two sample passages. First, Matthew's story of the stilling of the storm (Matthew 8.23–7), discussed in the previous chapter. In examining its theological potential, I pointed to its ecclesial dimension (especially when compared with Mark and Luke's parallel versions): the disciples/the Church being tossed about in a hostile world, and praying to the risen Lord in their midst. Luz's study of the reception history of this passage confirms that this ecclesial interpretation is very early (as early as Tertullian), and widespread throughout Christian history. The boat is the 'small ship of the Church' or 'Peter's little ship', which adds a further dimension to the Christological interpretation of the story (focusing on Christ as Lord over the elements).

But these are not the only readings of this story. Luz notes the distinctive reading of Peter Chrysologus, fifth-century Bishop of Ravenna. He reads the miracle as an allegory of the Christianizing of the city of Rome, the turbulent, infidel nations being tamed by Christ. Some later interpreters, perhaps indicative of the cultural shift from the communal to the individual, read the story in a more personal way: Christ entering 'the ship of our heart'.[95]

But the reception history of the stilling of the storm is not restricted to commentaries and other scholarly books. It has also influenced liturgical and devotional life. Generations of English-speaking Catholics have been brought up on the eucharistic hymn *Sweet Sacrament Divine*, by Francis Stanfield. Here the waters of the storm are interpreted as the cares and anxieties of the faithful, calmed by the risen Lord still present in the Eucharist:

> Save us, for still the tempest raves,
> save, lest we sink beneath the waves:
> sweet Sacrament of rest.

A second example is John's vision of Babylon in Revelation 17. The book of Revelation, given its dramatic, visual nature, has had a particularly rich reception history, and so we will need to be highly selective (further examples may be found in the fine volume on Revelation by Judith Kovacs and Christopher Rowland, in the BBC series).[96]

Most historical-critical commentators will identify Revelation's Babylon with imperial Rome, or Rome's personification in the goddess Roma (though some recognize that the Roman identification does not exhaust the meaning of this multivalent vision). When one turns to Revelation 17's reception history, this reading seems to be confirmed by some of the earliest interpreters, such as Tertullian and Hippolytus. However, below the surface, there is a profound difference. These patristic authors were reading Revelation as a persecuted minority in an age of martyrdom, with imperial Rome as the ruling power. For them, Babylon/Rome was indeed drunk with the blood of the martyrs. Thus theirs is a committed reading which contrasts sharply with the often detached interpretations of contemporary commentators (thus reception history asks about the relationship between interpretation and commitment).

But studying the reception history of Revelation 17 also throws up other possibilities. The emphasis on the wealth, luxury and idolatry of Babylon led to a broader patristic interpretation (found in Tertullian and Cyprian) which warned against the luxury and indulgence of the empire, and impacted on Church prescriptions about women's dress. One of the negative effects of this line of interpretation – especially in artistic representations – was the portrayal of the woman as the seductive whore (Babylon's identity as a city disappearing into the background).

More fruitful is the interpretation springing from Tyconius, according to which Babylon is 'the world' in opposition to the Church. This cuts the vision loose from being associated with one particular historical city, enabling it to speak to new generations and situations. It retains the prophetic edge of Revelation, giving the Church, especially where it is a threatened minority, a counter-cultural voice. Of course, it needs to be balanced by alternative voices within the New Testament, which are able to see the Spirit at work in societies and cultures beyond the boundaries of the Christian community.

Finally, there is the type of reading – common among certain Protestant interpreters though rooted in some Catholic medieval readings – which identifies Babylon not with ancient Rome but with papal Rome, or with individual popes. The validity of such a reading was explored in Chapter 1. It can be seen as an understandable reading in a particular historical context, with some roots in the text (which warns that some Christians might be too closely identified with Babylon). However, the negative effects of this anti-papal reading also need to be explored, not least in the bitter history of persecutions and martyrdoms which marked Christian life in England in the sixteenth and seventeenth centuries.[97]

To do

Select a passage from the New Testament, and find out as much as you can about its reception history (as well as the BBC, and the patristic resources mentioned in Chapter 10, web searches may help you to identify relevant material, including homiletic, artistic and musical interpretations). What different kinds of interpretation do you find? How effective have any of them been (both positively and negatively)? In what ways has your appreciation of the chosen passage been enlarged?

Painting the New Testament

A visit to any of our great art galleries, at home or abroad, should remind us of how important artists have been throughout history as interpreters of the Bible, especially the New Testament. Scenes from the gospels and from the Acts of the Apostles, wide-ranging visual interpretations of the person of Christ, and the dramatic visions of the book of Revelation can all be found. Nor have the epistles been excluded from artistic interest: there are depictions of Paul's visionary ascent (alluded to at 2 Corinthians 12), while artistic representations of Christ as the eternal High Priest are clearly influenced by the theology of the letter to the Hebrews.

The paintings of New Testament scenes in our art galleries are, however, for the most part 'out of context'. To understand them better, we should envisage them in their original context in churches and chapels, often over an altar or within a baptistery. It is this dimension which gives them their particular potency in engaging with the lives of the worshippers who view them in a liturgical context.

How might artists aid us in illuminating New Testament texts? A number of examples may help. Our first example is Piero della Francesca's *The Baptism of Christ* (*c.*1460, now in London's National Gallery), explored by John Drury in his excellent book *Painting the Word*.[98] It can be viewed on the National Gallery's website, at www.nationalgallery.org.uk/collection (its catalogue number is NG665). The story of the baptism, found in all three synoptic gospels, has often been explored as a crucial moment in the life of Jesus, or as a key scene for grasping the Christology of the individual evangelists. But how does this scene, and the baptism of John that underlies it, relate to the experience of those who view della Francesca's picture, or the Christian baptism many of them have received?

Though now in the National Gallery, John Drury reminds us of the original *Sitz im Leben* of della Francesca's *Baptism*: over the altar in the chapel of St John the Baptist, within the monastic church of the Camaldolese monks in Piero's hometown of Borgo San Sepolcro. In other words, it would have been viewed in a liturgical and sacramental setting, when the monks gathered for Mass. The two great sacraments of baptism and the Eucharist are brought together visually in its church setting.

This setting blurs the boundary between the historical event of Jesus' baptism in the Jordan, and the sacramental baptism experienced by the Christian worshipper. Della Francesca accentuates this identification between Christ and the baptized Christian, who has 'put on Christ', by the distinctive flesh colour he uses for two characters in the scene: Christ himself in the centre, and the man on the right who is pulling on his clothes after receiving John's baptism.

A further connection between this scene and the lives of the worshippers is made by the posture of Christ. It is a combination of prayerful stillness (appropriate to Camaldolese monks) and a forward movement, expressed by a tilt of the hips, as if Christ is moving towards us, or even moving us on.

There is one final dimension to della Francesca's portrayal worthy of note, which reaches forward to the end of the gospel story. Christ is naked apart from a loincloth, traditional in depictions of his crucifixion. It is a reminder that baptism is a death, and that Christ's own baptism will take place on Calvary. Yet the baptismal act is not complete without the new Christian rising with Christ. Hence one of the attendant angels holds a pink cloak, the same pink garment adorning Christ's resurrected body in della Francesca's *The Resurrection* (*c.* 1458).

Interestingly, this dramatic link between Christ's baptism and his death (and resurrection) is one which narrative critics have recently emphasized.[99] Their insights were anticipated 500 years earlier in artist-commentators like della Francesca, who made the further connection between these two scenes and the lives of contemporary viewers.

A second example is taken from Luke's infancy narrative (Luke 1—2), a popular tramping-ground for Western artists. Four Renaissance paintings inspired by Luke's narrative have been explored in a pioneering collaboration between an art historian, Heidi J. Hornik, and Mikeal C. Parsons, a New Testament scholar:[100] Leonardo da Vinci's *Uffizi Annunciation*, Jacopo Pontormo's *The Visitation*, Domenico Ghirlandaio's *Adoration of the Shepherds*, and Ambrogio Lorenzetti's *Presentation in the Temple*.

To take Ghirlandaio as our example (his painting can be viewed at the Web Gallery of Art: www.wga.hu), again Renaissance artists seem to have anticipated 'modern' and 'postmodern' critics in their insight into the text. His *Adoration of the Shepherds* (1483–5; also known by the longer title *The*

Nativity and Adoration of the Shepherds) was painted for an altarpiece in the Church of Santa Trinità in Florence. Among the features of Ghirlandaio's painting noted by Hornik, the following are especially worthy of note, as interpretations of Luke's story of Christ's birth and the shepherds:

- The child Jesus is resting on a sheaf of wheat, a symbol of the Eucharist (connections between the infant Christ's body and the eucharistic body were common in the medieval and Renaissance periods).
- The animals' trough, which becomes Christ's manger, is portrayed as a sarcophagus, echoing late medieval devotion to the Christ Child as a sacrifice. The sarcophagus picks up on a number of subtle echoes in Luke's narrative which could be taken as pointing towards Christ's future suffering and death (the lamb and the goldfinch in the picture are also symbols of Christ's passion). A contemporary narrative critic might pick up on the verbal and structural parallels between two scenes:

Luke 2.7:   'And she gave birth to her firstborn son
                    And wrapped him in bands of cloth,
                    And laid him in a manger . . .'

Luke 23.53: 'Then he took it [the body of Jesus] down,
                    Wrapped it in a linen cloth,
                    And laid it in a rock-hewn tomb . . .'

In both scenes a Joseph is involved: in the first, Joseph the husband of Mary, in the second, Joseph of Arimathea. A similar premonition of the passion in Luke's infancy story is found in the words of Simeon at 2.34–5.

Our final example is from the book of Revelation. The Trinity Apocalypse, so-called due to its current ownership by Trinity College, Cambridge, is an illuminated Apocalypse manuscript produced *c*.1250. Many think it was produced for Eleanor of Provence, Queen of Henry III of England. Eleanor's father had been influenced by the Apocalypse interpretation of the influential abbot Joachim of Fiore, and by Joachim's successors (for example, the Spiritual Franciscans) who saw the 'eternal gospel' of Revelation 14.6 as being proclaimed by the mendicant orders, especially the Franciscans.

Colour photographs of its illustrations can be found in *The Trinity Apocalypse*, edited by David McKitterick.[101] One scene is especially worthy of note: the battle between the saints and the beast from the sea (folio 14 verso; described at Revelation 13.7). Thirteenth-century readers of this illuminated Apocalypse would have been acutely aware of its contemporary relevance. Among the faithful battling with the seven-headed beast are a noble woman (possibly Queen Eleanor herself) and a Franciscan friar. The battle here is not understood as a first-century event of only historical interest, nor as an event of the eschatological future. Rather, it is a battle in which the contemporary Church is involved. Following the Joachite interpretation, St Francis's sons have a particular role to play here. But it also provokes the question for later generations: what role am I to play in the ongoing battle with the beast?

To do

Compare the way in which two different artists portray a scene from the gospels, Acts or Revelation. How have they responded to the New Testament text? Have they highlighted forgotten aspects in that text? What aspects of their own religious tradition have affected their portrayal? Do they engage in any way with their own contemporary situation (for example, political events and cultural trends)? Was their work commissioned (if so, by whom, and how might this have affected their portrayal)? What was the context in which it was intended to be viewed (for example, in church, in a private home, in a devotional book)?

The Contribution of Music

Non-literary interpretation of the New Testament is not confined to the visual. Musicians and hymn writers have also significantly influenced people's apprehension of the New Testament text. In this, they are building on the New Testament itself, which contains a number of early Christian hymns and canticles.

A glance through a standard hymn book will show the influence of the New Testament on Christian hymnody. Sometimes the dependence is quite straightforward, as in Timothy Dudley-Smith's rendering of the Magnificat (Luke 1.46–55), 'Tell out, my soul, the greatness of the Lord'. Sometimes, a more complex process of interpretation is at work. C. F. Alexander's Christmas carol 'Once in royal David's city', for example, juxtaposes Luke's marginal story of the Saviour placed in a manger (located in 'a lowly cattle shed') with the Johannine drama of the incarnation of the Logos ('He came down to earth from heaven'). But what binds these various strands together is the reception history of the Nativity story, in which Isaiah's ox and ass now worship at their master's crib (Isaiah 1.3). 'Alleluia, Sing to Jesus' is clearly influenced by the Christology of Hebrews when it says of Jesus: 'Thou within the veil hast entered, robed in flesh, our great High Priest'. Its genre as a communion hymn, however, offers a distinctly eucharistic interpretation of Hebrews (an interpretation hotly debated among New Testament scholars).

Composers have also regularly offered musical interpretations of gospel narratives, and sometimes whole New Testament books. The devotional life of many Christians, notably in the Lutheran tradition, has been influenced by the Passions of Johann Sebastian Bach (1685–1750), which interpret the various gospel narratives. These are regularly performed, often in a liturgical context, during Holy Week. Bach's *St Matthew Passion* illustrates his role as biblical interpreter, giving prominence to particular passages and characters:

- Bach has, for example, recreated musically Judas' horror at the realization of what he has done in betraying Jesus to the chief priests, and his cry of remorse is dramatically contrasted with the priestly chorus – 'But what is that to us? see thou, see thou to that, see thou to that' – while his throwing of the silver pieces into the temple treasury is represented by the rushing scales in the bass aria, 'Give, O give me back my Lord, give me, give, O give me back my Lord. See the silver, price of blood at your feet in horror pour'd.'
- So too he has highlighted the appearance of Pilate's wife (distinctive to Matthew's account), whose plea to her husband to have nothing to

do with Jesus is in stark contrast to the thunderous cry of the crowd: 'Barabbas'.

- Similarly, there is a dramatic change of tone at the point of Jesus' death, to mark the dramatic events surrounding the crucifixion of Jesus, which as it were crash into one another swiftly and violently: the rending of the temple curtain, the earthquake, the opening of the tombs, and the fear of the centurion and his companions.

The Apocalypse or book of Revelation particularly lends itself to musical performance, given its aural character and the number of canticles it contains. Handel's *Messiah* (1742) draws upon it for its 'Worthy is the Lamb that was slain' and the famous 'Hallelujah Chorus'.[102] Other composers to be inspired by the dramatic book include Olivier Messiaen (*Quartet for the End of Time,* composed in 1940 while he was a prisoner of war), and Gian Carlo Menotti. Some have attempted a musical setting of the whole Apocalypse, offering very different interpretations of the work: Franz Schmidt, *Das Buch mit Sieben Siegeln* (1938), Jean Françaix, *L'Apocalypse selon St Jean* (1939), Hilding Rosenberg, *The Revelation of St John* (Symphony No. 4, 1940), and John Tavener, *The Apocalypse* (1993).

Portraying Jesus in Film

The twentieth century made possible a new medium for New Testament interpretation: the cinema. Many will know the great Hollywood biblical epics, covering Old as well as New Testament themes, such as *The Ten Commandments.* Among depictions of New Testament stories and themes in film, pride of place must go to portrayals of Jesus. The so-called 'Celluloid Christ' has become an area of particular scholarly interest.

As well as more traditional 'Lives of Jesus', a number of films engage with a 'Christ-figure' who parallels Christ in his own life. An example of the latter is Denys Arcand's *Jesus of Montreal* (1989), in which the main character is a young actor playing the role of Jesus in a passion play; as the film progresses, the story of Christ's passion and death and his own life (and ultimate death) become increasingly intertwined.

Table 8: Significant Jesus-Films.

The King of Kings (Cecil B. DeMille, 1927 (silent))
King of Kings (Nicholas Ray, 1961)
The Gospel According to Saint Matthew (*Il Vangelo secondo Matteo*; Pier Paolo Pasolini, 1964)
The Greatest Story Ever Told (George Stevens, 1965)
Jesus Christ Superstar (film version; Norman Jewison, 1973)
Godspell (film version; David Greene, 1973)
Jesus of Nazareth (Franco Zeffirelli, 1977)
Jesus (US *The Jesus Film*; Peter Sykes and John Krish, 1979)
The Last Temptation of Christ (Martin Scorsese, 1988)
The Miracle Maker (animated; Stanislav Sokolov and Derek Hayes, 2000)
The Passion of the Christ (Mel Gibson, 2004)

A number of issues confront directors of a contemporary Jesus film (or are raised by a scholarly study of such films):

- Should one attempt to interpret one particular evangelist's story (for example, Pasolini's *Gospel According to St Matthew*), or aim at a harmonization of all four (typical of most Jesus films)? Or should one opt for a fictional narrative, perhaps following an existing novel (as in Scorsese's *Last Temptation of Christ*)?
- How should one portray Jesus? As a near contemporary capable of speaking to our concerns? As a Johannine stranger from heaven, verging at times on docetism (for example, Stevens' *The Greatest Story Ever Told*)? As another kind of stranger, one from an ancient society with ancient concerns? In his human capacity for empathy, human love and ability to change his mind?
- In answering this question, how far should one attend to the shifting sands of historical scholarship on 'Jesus' (with its range of 'historical Jesuses')? Which 'Jesus' should one adopt?

- Should one prefer a fresh interpretation, from where one stands (recognizing that all portraits of Jesus tell us much about the interpreter)?
- Should Jesus be viewed on screen from the front, or only from behind; or should the camera present the perspective of his own eyes, as he looks at the suffering of the sick, or summons the disciples from their boats?
- How much concern should there be for historical verisimilitude: for example, attempts in Zeffirelli's *Jesus of Nazareth* to evoke first-century Jewish and Roman Palestine (from the scenes in the synagogue to the clothing and headgear of the chief priests to Jesus carrying only the crossbeam to Calvary)? Or is this irrelevant in a fictional narrative, which conveys the director's interpretation of Jesus?
- How does one deal with the episodic nature of the gospels, where (apart from the passion narrative) scenes are not always linked together in a sequential manner (the earliest Jesus-films adopted this episodic approach, in contrast to the more coherent narratives with which most of us are more familiar).[103]
- In several of the gospels (notably Matthew and John) much space is devoted to Jesus' words rather than his actions. How is one to deal with this in a very different genre?
- Should one isolate one particular stage of Jesus' story from the rest (as in some of the earliest Jesus films, and Mel Gibson's *The Passion of the Christ*, which focus on the passion narrative: in Gibson's case, with flashbacks to episodes in the earlier story)? What are the implications of this?
- How far should one imitate one's predecessors? This is a reception-historical point: recognizing that Jesus films build on one another; just as they build on the whole history of Christian art and devotion (for example, Mel Gibson's *The Passion of the Christ* draws on the Stations of the Cross as well as Anne Catherine Emmerich's *The Dolorous Passion of our Lord Jesus Christ*, and paintings by artists such as Mantegna and Piero della Francesca).[104]
- How far should one attempt to convey the 'scandal' of the gospel? Is there any watering-down involved, for the sake of the intended audience?
- How should one deal with the portrayal of the Jewish authorities, and the Jewish people, in the retelling of the passion story (a live issue in scholarly study of the gospel passion narratives, and in Jewish–Christian dialogue).[105]

Reflection

If you were the director of a film about Jesus, how would you go about your task? What choices would you make between the various options expressed above? Ask yourself what has affected the choices you make.

Mark Goodacre's website *New Testament Gateway* has some excellent pages on Jesus in film (www.ntgateway.com/film). Three very different scholarly books on portrayals of Jesus in film are worth consulting:

- Lloyd Baugh, 1997, *Imaging the Divine: Jesus and Christ-Figures in Film*, Kansas City: Sheed and Ward.
- W. Barnes Tatum, 1998, *Jesus at the Movies: A Guide to the First Hundred Years*, Santa Rosa, CA: Polebridge Press.
- Richard Walsh, 2003, *Reading the Gospels in the Dark: Portrayals of Jesus in Film*, Harrisburg, London and New York: Trinity Press International.

To do

Watch either the crucifixion or the resurrection/post-resurrection scenes from two or three Jesus-films. How does each portray these scenes? In what ways do they differ, and why? What decisions have been taken in relation to the gospel narratives? Which of the depictions do you find the most satisfying, and which the least?

Are All Readings Valid?

The 'on-going' story of the New Testament texts, sometimes described as their 'afterlives', brings us back to a question which has been niggling throughout this studyguide: are all interpretations equally valid, or are some more valid than others? Are there some which are plain wrong? The series editors' preface to the Blackwell Bible Commentary states the intention of the volumes in the series to leave it to readers to 'make up their own minds on the value, morality, and validity of particular interpretations.'

How might one tackle this question of truth? Study of reception history, as well as a renewed interest in patristic and medieval exegesis, has challenged the view that texts only have one meaning. Nevertheless, in different ways, interpreters have wished to place constraints on the possibilities for interpretation. In his discussion of the effective history of Matthew's stilling of the storm story, for example, Ulrich Luz identifies three limits which he thinks ought to constrain interpretations of this story (constraints placed by the text itself):

- faith, springing from the risen Lord's lifting the doubter, is at the heart of the story;
- the story speaks of a community experience, that of the disciples, not merely a private experience or an event that only edifies the individual;
- the intertwining of God's help and human struggle rules out interpretations that regard discipleship as passive.[106]

A number of possible criteria present themselves for adjudicating between readings of New Testament passages:

- 'correspondence to the original meaning': taking the meaning for the original author as determinative in placing constraints on other meanings (though we have noted the difficulties involved in locating that 'original meaning' precisely);
- constraints in the text: detecting constraints in the text itself that rule out certain readings;
- a canonical criterion: judging readings according to a particular view of what is at the heart of the biblical or New Testament canon: for example, does a particular reading provoke 'love' (Luz)?[107] Does it correspond to the pattern of Jesus' life, death and resurrection as presented in the fourfold gospel (Kovacs and Rowland)?[108]
- an ethical criterion: readings that encourage injustice, or immoral actions such as genocide, should be rejected, even if they might be held to approximate to the perspective of the original author (for example, Fiorenza); this is closely connected with the canonical criterion;

- conformity to a particular position of faith: for example, patristic concern for readings to conform to the Rule of Faith; reading within a particular tradition of interpretation;
- criterion of commitment: preferring committed readings, or those which acknowledge a particular stance and interests, to those which claim detachment: for example, compare the persecuted Tertullian with historical-critical commentators in identifying Babylon with imperial Rome.

Further Reading

The *Blackwell Bible Commentary* series edited by John Sawyer, Judith Kovacs, Christopher Rowland and David M. Gunn (www.bbibcomm.net).

John Drury, 1999, *Painting the Word: Christian Pictures and their Meanings*, New Haven and London: Yale University Press/National Gallery Publications.

David Lyle Jeffrey (ed.), 1992, *A Dictionary of Biblical Tradition in English Literature*, Grand Rapids, Michigan: Eerdmans.

Ulrich Luz, 1994, *Matthew in History: Interpretation, Influence, and Effects*, Minneapolis: Fortress Press.

12

Putting It Into Practice

The Beheading of John the Baptist

The aim of this final chapter is to put into practice lessons learned from the rest of the book, attempting to comment on a passage in different ways, asking the different types of questions raised by different approaches. A passage from Matthew's Gospel (the Beheading of John the Baptist, Matthew 14.1–12) has been selected by way of illustration. It is hoped this example will encourage you to read and interpret further passages yourself.

1 At that time Herod the ruler heard reports about Jesus;

2 and he said to his servants, 'This is John the Baptist; he has been raised from the dead, and for this reason these powers are at work in him.'

3 For Herod had arrested John, bound him, and put him in prison on account of Herodias, his brother Philip's wife,

4 because John had been telling him, 'It is not lawful for you to have her.'

5 Though Herod wanted to put him to death, he feared the crowd, because they regarded him as a prophet.

6 But when Herod's birthday came, the daughter of Herodias danced before the company, and she pleased Herod

7 so much that he promised on oath to grant her whatever she might ask.

8 Prompted by her mother, she said, 'Give me the head of John the Baptist here on a platter.'

9 The king was grieved, yet out of regard for his oaths and for the guests, he commanded it to be given;

10 he sent and had John beheaded in the prison.

11 The head was brought on a platter and given to the girl, who brought it to her mother.

12 His disciples came and took the body and buried it; then they went and told Jesus.

Establishing the Text

Textual Criticism

There are few text-critical issues to do with this passage (see footnotes in English study editions, or marginal notes in Greek New Testaments).[109]

- In verse 3, some manuscripts read simply 'his brother's wife' instead of 'his brother Philip's wife': the latter is probably original, given that it is the harder reading (it contradicts the account in Josephus, *Antiquities* 18.5.4, which states that Herodias was the wife of another brother, also called Herod). A scribe would have omitted 'Philip' as a correction (as also in the shorter text of Luke 3.19). Alternatively, 'Philip' may have been added in order to harmonize Matthew with Mark 6.17.
- In verse 9, some scribes seem to have altered the text in order to clarify an existing ambiguity: does the 'out of regard for his oaths' qualify what precedes ('The king was grieved') or what follows ('he commanded [John's head] to be given')? The apparent scribal alterations opt for the latter.

English Translation

Similarly, there are few issues for the English translator, apart from verse 9 (though it would be worth comparing two or three different versions):

- Though most translate the technical term 'tetrarch' (*tetraarchēs*, 'ruler of a fourth') to describe Herod in verse 1, some use the non-technical 'ruler', while the occasional translator misleadingly translates the word as 'king'.

Historical-Critical Questions

This passage can be found, with its synoptic parallels, at Aland §144 or Throckmorton §110–11.

Source Criticism

Matthew's narrative (actually two connected pericopae, verses 1–2 and verses 3–12) has a direct parallel at Mark 6.14–29, and a partial parallel at Luke 9.7–9 (cf. Luke 3.19–20, where John's arrest by Herod is recounted prior to Jesus' baptism). Matthew and Mark are very similar, though with some differences:

- Mark 6.15–16 contrasts Herod's identification of Jesus with the now-dead John with alternative suggestions of others: Elijah or one of the prophets.
- Mark is incorrect in calling Herod a 'king'; Matthew correctly calls him a 'tetrarch' (at least in verse 1!).
- Matthew's version is significantly shorter than Mark's (for example, he omits reference to the groups invited to the birthday party and lacks the dialogue between Herod and the daughter).
- Matthew's account is simpler: in contrast to Mark, who has Herodias wanting John killed and Herod fearing John and protecting him (thus highlighting a clash within the marriage), Matthew has Herod wanting to kill John, though fearing the people.

How is one best to account for the synoptic relationship? Is the shorter account (Matthew's) to be regarded as earlier, expanded by Mark? In this case, a better case can be found for Marcan priority, on the basis of 'evangelistic fatigue':[110]
- Matthew's shortened version can be well explained as an attempt to abbreviate Mark's longer account, and in the process correcting errors Mark made (for example, calling Herod a 'king' rather than a 'tetrarch').
- But as the story progresses, there are three indications that Matthew is suffering from fatigue and lapses into following his source:
  - (1) in verse 9, he follows Mark in calling Herod a 'king', despite having previously correctly called him a 'tetrarch';
  - (2) also in verse 9, he seems to have forgotten his earlier abbreviation of

the story (Herod himself wants John killed), for he now puzzling says that 'the king was sorry' or 'grieved';

(3) when he gets to the end of the story, he seems to have forgotten that this is a recounted 'flash-back' to a past event, and continues as if it had happened in narrative time.

Form Criticism

- What kind of story is this? It has a rather unusual form compared with other pericopae in the gospel tradition. It is a popular tale (compare the report in Josephus), rather than a particularly Christian story.
- Its original *Sitz im Leben* may have been in the popular gossip of first-century Palestinian Jews. However, in its current form, it has a particular edge – appropriate for Christian teaching – in recounting the martyrdom of a prophet.
- The form may have been shaped by Old Testament antecedents: the story of Jezebel (1 Kings 21) in the portrayal of Herodias, and the book of Esther (Esther 1; 5.3: 'What is your request? It shall be given you, even to the half of my kingdom'). However, the echoes are less pronounced in Matthew than in Mark, who gives more prominence to Herodias.

Redaction Criticism

If (as argued above) Matthew is using Mark as his source, it is easier to see the changes he has made, which may point to his particular concerns. These changes raise questions such as these:

- By giving more attention to John rather than to Herod (compare Mark), is Matthew wanting to highlight John's role as a prophet, Elijah returned?
- What is the significance of Matthew apparently making Herod the villain (as in Josephus, contra Mark)?
- How does the account of John's death here relate to what Matthew wants to say about Jesus?

Further Historical Background

In order to appreciate the thrust of the story, further historical background information may be helpful.

- You may want to identify 'Herod the Tetrarch' (Herod Antipas, son of Herod the Great), and learn more about his role in first-century Palestinian politics.
- Some knowledge of the territory governed by Herod Antipas may serve to explain his interest in both the Galilean Jesus and John, baptizing in the Jordan valley (consulting a Bible atlas will clarify geographical questions).
- Interestingly, there is an alternative account of John's demise in the writings of the Jewish historian Flavius Josephus (*Antiquities* 18.5.2), which offers a useful point of comparison.

Literary Questions

Here are just a sample of the literary questions which this story raises:

- What is one to make of the juxtaposition of this story with what precedes (Jesus' rejection by his own people in Nazareth, Matthew 13.54–8)?
- Similarly, how does it relate to what follows (the feeding of the five thousand, Matthew 14.13–21)? What is the difference between the two banquets?
- How does this story fit into the narrative as a whole, and its unfolding plot? How, for example, does it anticipate Jesus' fate? What has been said about John, and his imprisonment, already in Matthew's narrative?
- How is the implied reader expected to respond to this story? For example, she might especially note the parallel between 14.12 (John's disciples came and took his body and buried it) and 27.57–60, where Joseph, a disciple of Jesus, obtains his body and places it in a tomb. She might also detect the contrast, however, between the disciples of John, who go and tell Jesus of a death (of John, who was only thought to have been raised from the dead,

verse 2), and the women at the tomb, who go away to tell Jesus' disciples of a genuine resurrection (Matthew 28.7–11).
- How are the various characters portrayed? Who is the protagonist, and who the antagonist(s)? How is the implied reader expected to respond to the 'crowd'?
- What is the function of the story being 'out of sequence' in terms of narrative time?

Social-Scientific Questions

Reading the story again from a social-scientific perspective might throw up additional issues:

- Herod's interest in Jesus' 'powers' has a more sinister slant in a society focused on honour and shame: Herod wants to know where Jesus fits, in relation to him, in the power hierarchy.[111]
- Similarly, shame is involved in the portrayal of a royal princess dancing in public.
- The social role of women as opposed to men in ancient society is reflected in the private, 'behind-the-scenes' activity of Herodias.
- The socio-economic dynamic between Herod, Herodias and her daughter, on the one hand, and John and the crowd, on the other, is an implicit feature of the story.

Issues Raised by Perspective

Reading this story from different perspectives will raise a host of other issues:

- What are we to make of the portrayals of Herodias and her daughter? Do they, or do their subsequent interpretations, stereotype the feminine from a male's perspective? Should Herodias and her daughter become more central to a reading of the story?

- Where is authentic power to be located in this 'power play': in Herod's 'kingdom' or in the alternative kingdom represented by John? How does this story challenge our own power games?
- How does this story speak to others who, in their own day, feel called to stand up prophetically to the ruling classes?
- Some might focus on the economic dimension of this story: the contrast between the luxury and extravagance of Herod's banquet, and the simplicity and equality of the feeding of the five thousand which follows it.

Theological Issues

Reflecting upon this passage, and grappling with it theologically, will raise issues such as these:

- How am I being invited to reassess my understanding of God in this story which presents the suffering and death of one of God's servants at the hands of a powerful antagonist?
- Is God only to be understood as on the side of John? Might the story itself submit to a theological critique?
- How might this passage be calling me to respond, in recounting the story of a martyred prophet like John? What demands are being made on me? What might a prophetic ministry look like today?

Reception History

Finally, attention to the reception history of this story, and its wider effects (positive and negative), might open up other possibilities:

- There is patristic interest in the characters of Herod and Herodias, and the motives they exemplify.
- Luz's review of the story's effective history notes considerable focus on the daughter of Herodias, identified as Salome: notable focus is on the indecent and seductive nature of her dance (and its wider implications

for Christian living), though other aspects of the girl's character are later expressed (for example, Oscar Wilde's 1893 play *Salome* and Richard Strauss's opera of the same name).[112]

- John Chrysostom's homily on the story focuses on wider moral concerns. He interprets it as a warning to both women *and* men about the unseemliness, extravagance and drunkenness associated with weddings (*Homilies on St Matthew* 48). But there is more depth to Chrysostom's homily: it betrays a concern for the poor and encouragement for those who, like John, suffer injustice at the hands of the powerful.
- A large number of artists have interpreted aspects of this story visually: for example, Salome's dance, John's beheading, or the presentation of John's head to Herod or to Salome (there are several depictions of various aspects of this scene in the National Gallery: see www.nationalgallery.org.uk).

Notes

Chapter 1 Introducing the New Testament

1 John Goldingay, 1994, *Models for Scripture*, Grand Rapids, Michigan: Eerdmans.
2 See especially Luke Timothy Johnson and William S. Kurz SJ, 2002, *The Future of Catholic Biblical Scholarship: A Constructive Conversation*, Grand Rapids, Michigan: Eerdmans; Ellen F. Davis and Richard B. Hays (eds), 2003, *The Art of Reading Scripture*, Grand Rapids, Michigan/Cambridge: Eerdmans.

Chapter 2 Where is Meaning to be Found?

3 Mark Allan Powell, 2001, *Chasing the Eastern Star: Adventures in Biblical Reader-Response Criticism*, Louisville, Kentucky: Westminster John Knox Press, pp. 22–7.
4 A good introduction is Mark A. Powell, 1993, *What is Narrative Criticism?* London: SPCK.
5 L. William Countryman, 2003, *Interpreting the Truth: Changing the Paradigm of Biblical Studies*, Harrisburg: Trinity Press International, pp. 16–41.
6 On this, see Powell, *Chasing the Eastern Star*, pp. 57–74.
7 Good examples of the reception history of individual New Testament books can be found in the *Blackwell Bible Commentary* (www.bbibcomm.net).
8 The reception history of this vision is explored further in Ian Boxall, 2001, 'The Many Faces of Babylon the Great: *Wirkungsgeschichte* and the Interpretation of Revelation 17', in Steve Moyise (ed.), *Studies in the Book of Revelation*, Edinburgh and New York: T. & T. Clark, pp. 51–68.

Chapter 3 The Jesus Effect

9 Gerd Theissen, 1987, *The Shadow of the Galilean*, ET London: SCM Press.

10 For different views on the gospel passion narratives, whether they represent 'prophecy historicized' or 'history remembered', see R. E. Brown, 1994, *The Death of the Messiah*, London: Geoffrey Chapman, especially volume 1, pp. 4–35, and John Dominic Crossan, 1995, *Who Killed Jesus?* New York: Harper Collins.

11 Luke Timothy Johnson, 1999, *The Writings of the New Testament: An Interpretation*, rev. edn, London: SCM Press, p. 141.

12 James D. G. Dunn, 2005, *A New Perspective on Jesus: What the Quest for the Historical Jesus Missed*, Grand Rapids, Michigan: Baker Academic, especially pp. 46–56 and pp. 89–101. A fuller account of Dunn's thesis can be found in his 2003 *Jesus Remembered*, Grand Rapids, Michigan/Cambridge: Eerdmans.

13 Raymond E. Brown, 1994, *An Introduction to New Testament Christology*, London: Geoffrey Chapman.

14 For a brief discussion, see Larry W. Hurtado, 2005, *How on Earth Did Jesus Become a God?* Grand Rapids, Michigan/Cambridge: Eerdmans. This is a summary of his more substantial treatment in his 2003 *Lord Jesus Christ: Devotion to Jesus in Earliest Christianity*, Grand Rapids, Michigan/Cambridge: Eerdmans. For alternative views, see e.g. Maurice Casey, 1991, *From Jewish Prophet to Gentile God*, Louisville: Westminster John Knox; James D. G. Dunn, 1980, *Christology in the Making*, London: SCM.

Chapter 4 Determining the Text

15 An accessible introduction to New Testament textual criticism is Keith Elliott and Ian Moir, 1995, *Manuscripts and the Text of the Greek New Testament*, Edinburgh: T. & T. Clark.

16 On this see Bruce Chilton, 1986, *Beginning New Testament Study*, London: SPCK, pp. 96–101.

Chapter 5 Why Four Gospels?

17 See e.g. Tom Thatcher, 2006, *Why John Wrote a Gospel: Jesus – Memory – History*, Louisville, Kentucky: Westminster John Knox Press.

18 E.g. Graham Stanton, 1995, *Gospel Truth? New Light on Jesus and the Gospels*, London: HarperCollins, pp. 11–19.

19 Translation from Alexander Roberts and James Donaldson (eds), 1995, *The Ante-Nicene Fathers*, Peabody, Massachusetts: Hendrickson, vol. 1, p. 428.

20 See Graham Stanton, 2004, *Jesus and Gospel*, Cambridge: Cambridge University Press, pp. 9–62.

21 Charles H. Talbert, 1978, *What is a Gospel? The Genre of the Canonical Gospels*, London: SPCK; Richard A. Burridge, 2004, *What are the Gospels? A Comparison with Graeco-Roman Biography*, 2nd edition, Grand Rapids, Michigan/Cambridge: Eerdmans (first edition published 1992).

22 J. Louis Martyn, 1968, *History and Theology in the Fourth Gospel*, New York: Harper & Row; Raymond E. Brown, 1979, *The Community of the Beloved Disciple*, London: Geoffrey Chapman. See also John Ashton, 1991, *Understanding the Fourth Gospel*, Oxford: Clarendon Press.

23 Richard Bauckham (ed.), 1998, *The Gospels for All Christians: Rethinking the Gospel Audiences*, Edinburgh: T. & T. Clark.

24 E.g. Philip Esler, 1998, 'Community and Gospel in Early Christianity: A Response to Richard Bauckham's *Gospels for All Christians*', *Scottish Journal of Theology* 51: 235–48, followed by a response from Richard Bauckham (pp. 249–53); David C. Sim, 2001, 'The Gospels for All Christians: A Response to Richard Bauckham,' *Journal for the Study of the New Testament* 84: 3–27; Edward W. Klink III, 2004, 'The Gospel Community Debate: State of the Question,' *Currents in Biblical Research* 3.1: 60–85.

25 Barbara Shellard, 2002, *New Light on Luke: Its Purpose, Sources and Literary Context*, JSNT Supplement Series 215; London: Sheffield Academic Press.

Chapter 6 Reading Historically

26 Paula Fredriksen, 2000, *Jesus of Nazareth, King of the Jews*, London: Macmillan, pp. 42–50.

27 The classic work is Rudolf Bultmann, 1963, *The History of the Synoptic Tradition*, ET Oxford: Basil Blackwell.

28 Luke Timothy Johnson, 1999, *The Writings of the New Testament: An Interpretation*, revised edition; London: SCM Press, pp. 142–3.

29 Bultmann, *History of the Synoptic Tradition*, pp. 14f.

30 Günther Bornkamm, Gerhard Barth and Heinz Joachim Held, 1963, *Tradition and Interpretation in Matthew*, ET London: SCM Press; Willi Marxsen, 1969, *Mark the Evangelist*, ET Nashville and New York: Abingdon Press; Hans Conzelmann, 1960, *The Theology of St Luke*, ET London: Faber & Faber.

31 Morna Hooker, 1983, *The Message of Mark*, London: Epworth Press, p. 3.

Chapter 7 Literary Readings

32 Mark Allen Powell, *Chasing the Eastern Star*, p. 3.

33 A. Katherine Grieb, 2002, *The Story of Romans: A Narrative Defense of God's Righteousness*, Louisville, Kentucky/London: Westminster John Knox Press.

34 J. D. Kingsbury, 1986, *Matthew As Story*, Philadelphia: Fortress Press, p. 38.

35 Francis J. Moloney, 2004, *Mark: Storyteller, Interpreter, Evangelist*, Peabody, Massachusetts: Hendrickson, pp. 48–54.

36 For this reading of the story, see e.g. Gerd Theissen, *The Shadow of the Galilean*, p. 106.

37 On this see e.g. Steve Moyise, 2001, *The Old Testament in the New: An Introduction*, London and New York: Continuum, pp. 1–8.

38 Richard B. Hays, 1989, *Echoes of Scripture in the Letters of Paul*, New Haven and London: Yale University Press.

39 George A. Kennedy, 1984, *New Testament Interpretation through Rhetorical Criticism*, Chapel Hill, NC/London: University of North Carolina Press.

40 Hans Dieter Betz, 1979, *Galatians*, Hermeneia; Philadelphia: Fortress Press.

Chapter 8 Social-Scientific Readings

41 Quoted in John Elliott, 1993, *Social-Scientific Criticism of the New Testament*, London: SPCK, p. 59.

42 Bruce J. Malina, 1981, *The New Testament World: Insights from Cultural Anthropology*, Atlanta: John Knox Press (UK edition published by SCM Press in 1983).

43 Malina, *New Testament World*, p. 55.

44 See Malina, *New Testament World*. Philip Esler provides some other examples of how these might impact on the New Testament texts in his 1994 *The First Christians in their Social Worlds*, London: Routledge, pp. 19–36.

45 Wayne Meeks, 1983, *The First Urban Christians*, New Haven and London: Yale University Press; Gerd Theissen, 1982, *The Social Setting of Pauline Christianity*, Minneapolis: Fortress Press.

46 Theissen, *Social Setting of Pauline Christianity*, p. 40.

47 John Chow, 1992, *Patronage and Power: A Study of Social Networks in Corinth*, JSNT Supplement Series 75; Sheffield: Sheffield Academic Press.

48 Meeks, *First Urban Christians*, pp. 140–63.

Chapter 9 Acknowledging One's Commitments

49 Elisabeth Schüssler Fiorenza, 1983, *In Memory of Her: A Feminist Theological Reconstruction of Christian Origins*, London: SCM Press.

50 Janice Capel Anderson, 2001, 'Matthew: Gender and Reading', in Amy-Jill Levine (ed.), *A Feminist Companion to Matthew*, Feminist Companion to the New Testament and Early Christian Writings 1; Sheffield: Sheffield Academic Press, pp. 25–51.

51 E.g. Fiorenza, *In Memory of Her*, pp. 140–51.

52 Fiorenza, *In Memory of Her*, p. 167.

53 Gail R. O'Day, 2001, 'Surprised by Faith: Jesus and the Canaanite Woman', in Amy-Jill Levine (ed.), *A Feminist Companion to Matthew*, pp. 114–25.

54 O'Day, 'Surprised by Faith', p. 125.

55 See e.g. F. Scott Spencer, 2003, '"You Just Don't Understand" (Or Do You?): Jesus, Women and Conversation in the Fourth Gospel', in Amy-Jill Levine (ed.), *A Feminist Companion to John* vol. 1, Feminist Companion to the New Testament and Early Christian Writings 4; London and New York: Sheffield Academic Press, pp. 40–5.

56 Christopher Rowland and Mark Corner, 1989, *Liberating Exegesis: The Challenge of Liberation Theology to Biblical Studies*, Louisville, Kentucky: Westminster John Knox Press.

57 Rowland and Corner, *Liberating Exegesis*, pp. 37–42.

58 Ernesto Cardenal (ed.), 1977–1984, *The Gospel in Solentiname*, 4 vols, Maryknoll, NY: Orbis Books.

59 Elsa Tamez, 2002, *The Scandalous Message of James*, revised edition, New York: Crossroad.

60 Tamez, *Scandalous Message*, p. 1.

61 Daniel Patte, J. Severino Croatto, Nicole Wilkinson Duran, Teresa Okure and Archie Chi Chung Lee (eds), 2004, *Global Bible Commentary*, Nashville: Abingdon Press.

62 Alejandro Duarte, 'Matthew', in Patte et al., *Global Bible Commentary*, pp. 350–60.

63 Justin Ukpong, 'Luke', in Patte et al., *Global Bible Commentary*, pp. 385–94.

64 Ukpong, 'Luke', p. 391.

65 R. S. Sugirtharajah, 1998, 'Biblical Studies after the Empire: From A Colonial to a Postcolonial Mode of Interpretation,' in R. S. Sugirtharajah (ed.), *The Postcolonial Bible*, Sheffield: Sheffield Academic Press, p. 16.

66 R. S. Sugirtharajah, 2005, 'Scripture, Scholarship, Empire: Putting the Discipline in its Place', *Expository Times* 117 (October), p. 7.

67 R. S. Sugirtharajah, 2003, *Postcolonial Reconfigurations: An Alternative Way of Reading the Bible and Doing Theology*, London: SCM Press, pp. 103–9.

68 Sugirtharajah, *Postcolonial Reconfigurations*, pp. 21–7.

69 Joseph Enuwosa, 2005, 'African Cultural Hermeneutics: Interpreting the New Testament in a Cultural Context', *Black Theology: An International Journal* 3.1: 86–98.

70 Richard Bauckham, 1999, *James*, New Testament Readings; London and New York: Routledge, pp. 14–16.

71 Nicholas King SJ, 1995, *Setting the Gospel Free*, Pietermaritzburg: Cluster Publications, p. 8.

Chapter 10 The New Testament and the Question of God

72 Jerome H. Neyrey, 2004, *Render to God: New Testament Understandings of the Divine*, Minneapolis: Fortress Press.

73 Augustine, 1873, *Lectures or Tractates on the Gospel according to St John*, trans. J. Gibb, Edinburgh: T. & T. Clark, p. 9 (Tractate I.12).

74 An accessible English translation of Origen's *Commentary on the Gospel of St John* can be found at www.newadvent.org/fathers/1015.htm.

75 Cited from J. L. Houlden (ed.), 1995, *The Interpretation of the Bible in the Church*, London: SCM Press, p. 3.

76 A slightly abridged version of Augustine, *Quaestiones Evangeliorum*, II, 19: cited in C. H. Dodd, 1942, *The Parables of the Kingdom*, 3rd edn; London: Religious Book Club, pp. 11f.

77 Johnson and Kurz, *The Future of Catholic Biblical Scholarship*, pp. 47–60.

78 Brian E. Daley SJ, 2003, 'Is Patristic Exegesis Still Usable? Some Reflections on Early Christian Interpretation of the Psalms', in Ellen F. Davis and Richard B. Hays (eds), *The Art of Reading Scripture*, Grand Rapids, Michigan/Cambridge: Eerdmans, pp. 69–88.

79 Powell, *Chasing the Eastern Star*, p. 51.

80 John Ashton, 2000, *The Religion of Paul the Apostle*, New Haven and London: Yale University Press.

81 Christopher Rowland and Christopher Tuckett (eds), 2006, *The Nature of New Testament Theology*, Oxford: Blackwell.

82 On this see e.g. Luke Timothy Johnson, 'Does a Theology of the Canonical Gospels Make Sense?' in Rowland and Tuckett, *The Nature of New Testament Theology*, pp. 93–108.

83 William Wrede, 'The Task and Methods of "New Testament Theology",' in

Robert Morgan (ed.), 1973, *The Nature of New Testament Theology*, London: SCM Press, p. 84.

84 Heikki Räisänen, 1990, *Beyond New Testament Theology*, ET London/ Philadelphia: SCM Press/Trinity Press International.

85 An accessible introduction to *lectio divina* is David Foster OSB, 2005, *Reading with God: Lectio Divina*, London and New York: Continuum.

86 Foster, *Reading with God*, p. 43.

87 John Chrysostom, *Homilies on St Matthew*, 25.

88 Michel de Verteuil, 2004, *Lectio Divina with the Sunday Gospels: the Year of Luke – Year C*, Blackrock: Columba Press, p. 7. De Verteuil has produced three volumes covering the three-year Roman Catholic Sunday lectionary (Matthew, Mark as well as Luke), from the perspective of *lectio divina*.

89 Foster, *Reading with God*, pp. 114–16.

Chapter 11 The Ongoing Story

90 For an interesting article exploring this theme, see James C. Howell, 'Christ Was Like St Francis', in Davis and Hays (eds), *The Art of Reading Scripture*, pp. 89–108.

91 Ulrich Luz, 'The Contribution of Reception History to a Theology of the New Testament', in Rowland and Tuckett (eds), *The Nature of New Testament Theology*, p. 126.

92 Ulrich Luz, 1990, *Matthew 1–7: A Commentary*, ET Edinburgh: T. & T. Clark; also his 1994 *Matthew in History: Interpretation, Influence, and Effects*, Minneapolis: Fortress Press; 2005, *Studies in Matthew*, Grand Rapids, Michigan/Cambridge: Eerdmans.

93 Luz in Rowland and Tuckett, *The Nature of New Testament Theology*, pp. 124–6.

94 For the visual impact of such anti-Semitic readings of the passion narratives, see Heinz Schreckenberg, 1996, *The Jews in Christian Art: An Illustrated History*, ET London: SCM Press.

95 Ulrich Luz, 2001, *Matthew 8–20*, ET Hermeneia; Minneapolis: Fortress Press, pp. 15–22.

96 Judith Kovacs and Christopher Rowland, 2004, *Revelation: the Apocalypse of Jesus Christ*, Blackwell Bible Commentaries; Oxford: Blackwell.

97 For further details, see Ian Boxall, 'The Many Faces of Babylon the Great: *Wirkungsgeschichte* and the Interpretation of Revelation 17', pp. 51–68.

98 John Drury, 1999, *Painting the Word: Christian Pictures and their Meanings*, New Haven and London: Yale University Press/National Gallery Publications.

Other useful books on Christian art include: Helen de Borchgrave, 1999, *A Journey into Christian Art*, Oxford: Lion Publishing; Robin Margaret Jensen, 2000, *Understanding Early Christian Art*, London and New York: Routledge; Richard Harries, 2004, *The Passion in Art*, Aldershot: Ashgate.

99 See for example, in relation to Mark's Gospel, Donald H. Juel, 1994, *A Master of Surprise*, Minneapolis: Fortress Press, pp. 33–43.

100 Heidi J. Hornik and Mikeal C. Parsons, 2003, *Illuminating Luke: The Infancy Narrative in Italian Renaissance Painting*, Harrisburg, London and New York: Trinity Press International.

101 David McKitterick (ed.), 2005, *The Trinity Apocalypse*, London and Toronto: British Library and Toronto University Press. Selected images can also be found in Frederick van der Meer, 1978, *Apocalypse: Visions from the Book of Revelation in Western Art*, ET London: Thames and Hudson, chapter 10.

102 See Roger A. Bullard, 1993, *Messiah: The Gospel according to Handel's Oratorio*, Grand Rapids, Michigan: Eerdmans.

103 Lloyd Baugh, 1997, *Imaging the Divine: Jesus and Christ-Figures in Film*, Kansas City: Sheed and Ward, pp. 7–10.

104 For scholarly discussion of Gibson's film, see Kathleen E. Corley and Robert L. Webb (eds), 2004, *Jesus and Mel Gibson's The Passion of the Christ: the Film, the Gospels and the Claims of History*, London and New York: Continuum.

105 On the anti-Semitism or anti-Judaism of Gibson's *The Passion of the Christ*, see the rather different assessments by John Dominic Crossan and Mark Goodacre in Corley and Webb, *Jesus and Mel Gibson's The Passion of the Christ*, pp. 8–44.

106 Luz, *Matthew 8–20*, p. 22.

107 See Luz, *Matthew in History*, chapter 5.

108 Kovacs and Rowland, *Revelation*, p. 248.

Chapter 12 Putting It Into Practice

109 Those with Greek might want to consult Bruce M. Metzger, 1971, *A Textual Commentary on the Greek New Testament*, Stuttgart: United Bible Societies, pp. 35–6.

110 On this, see Mark Goodacre, 1998, 'Fatigue in the Synoptics', *New Testament Studies* 44: 45–58. This article may be accessed on the web at www.ntgateway.com/Q/fatigue.htm.

111 For more on this, see Bruce J. Malina and Richard L. Rohrbaugh, 2003, *Social-Science Commentary on the Synoptic Gospels*, 2nd edition; Minneapolis: Fortress Press.

112 See Luz, *Matthew 8–20*, pp. 308–9.

Index of Bible References

23	34	6.6b—8.30	117	7.27	88
24—25	117	6.14–29	195–6	7.31–35	26, 29
24.36	60	6.17	194	7.32	25, 26
24.51	121	6.45—8.10	98	8.26–39	119
25.30	121	6.45	98	8.26	60
26—27	186–7	6.45–52	103	9.7–9	195
26.26–29	52	6.47–52	49	10.25–37	164
26.53	154	6.53	99	11.2–4	51
26.68	84	7.19	118	12.35–40	175
27.45–54	80	7.24–30	30	15.11–32	146
27.49	64	8	119	16.19–31	153
27.57–60	197	8.31	117	19.45–48	50
28.7–11	198	9.9–13	89	21.38	60
28.20	119	10.38	121	22.14–23	52
		11.12–26	109	22.20	13
Mark		11.15–19	50	22.64	84
1—2	107	13.14	11, 57	23.44–8	80
1.1	59, 63, 77,	13.32	60	23.53	184
	88, 117	14.9	148	24	16
1.1–13	117	14.22–5	52	24.27	54
1.2	9	14.36	51		
1.2–6	87–8	15.16–20	118	**John**	
1.8	59	15.33–9	80	1	51, 96
1.9	39	15.37–9	121	1.1–18	52, 161–3
1.9–11	42–4, 121,	15.38	42	1.19–23	87, 90
	182–3	16.1–4	117	1.1	39
1.14—8.30	117	16.1–8	117	1.3–4	65
1.14—3.6	117	16.8	11, 60, 63	1.16	162
1.14–15	117	16.9–20	63	2.4	71
1.29–31	92			2.13–22	50
1.41	60	**Luke**		3	90, 118
2.1—3.6	108	1	51	3.3	72
2.1–12	106	1—2	147, 183–4	4	147
2.18–22	14	1.1–4	32, 72, 83	4.9	10, 59,
2.22	15	1.46–55	186		130–1
2.23–8	99–102	2.7	184	4.10	72
2.27	119	2.34–35	184	4.32	118
3.1–6	117	2.41–51	51	4.46–54	119
3.7—6.6a	117	3	107, 130	5.3–4	64
3.7–12	117	3.1–6	87, 89	7.36	60
3.20–21	109	3.19	194	7.53—8.11	60
3.20–35	108, 132	3.19–20	42, 195	8.32	37
3.31–5	109	3.21–22	42–4, 182–3	14	119
4.35—6.44	98	4.5–12	109	14—17	124
4.35—5.1	118	4.22	64	16	119
5.1	60	5.33–39	14	19.28–30	80
5.1–20	155	5.39	15	20.1–18	149–51
5.21–43	109	6.1–5	99–102	21.1–8	72
6.3	63	7.1–10	106, 119	21.24–25	95

Index of Subjects

Africa, African readings 62, 154–8, 162
allegorical readings 82, 163–7, 168, 170, 180
Anglican tradition 51, 154
anti-Semitism, anti-Jewish 13–15, 34, 53–4,
   90, 117, 178, 189
Aramaic 51, 53, 71, 82, 104
archaeology 23, 92–6, 110–11, 126, 136
Armenia, Armenian 7, 8, 58
art, artists 12, 16, 23, 79, 80, 112–13, 149,
   176, 177, 179, 181, 182–5, 189, 200
audience, audiences 12, 29, 32, 34, 37, 47, 67,
   78, 81–2, 94–6, 104, 122, 123–5, 146, 189
Augustinian Hypothesis   84, 86
author-centred readings 26–7, 28–9, 32–33,
   36, 94–111, 195–7
authorial intention 28, 32–4, 36–8, 94–5,
   114, 166
authority of Scripture 16–17

bible atlas 2, 97, 157, 197
British Library 6, 8, 20

canon 8, 14, 20–3, 74, 75–8, 84, 157, 168,
   172, 191
canonical order 20–2, 84
characterization, characters 29, 33, 34, 117,
   118–19, 120, 147, 155, 183, 186, 187, 198,
   199
Christology 42–5, 48–50, 52–3, 54, 60, 65–
   6, 79, 96, 126, 162–3, 170–1, 179, 182–3,
   186, 187–9
Codex Alexandrinus 58, 64
Codex Bezae 22, 58, 59, 64
Codex Sinaiticus 20–22, 58, 59, 63, 64
Codex Vaticanus 58, 63, 64
commentaries 2, 3, 61, 64, 67, 124, 132, 142,
   151, 154, 155, 161–5, 167, 176–7, 179, 190
community of readers 30–1, 36, 47, 168–9
composition criticism 94, 108

Coptic 58, 62
cultural anthropology 127, 128, 129–32

dating of New Testament books 18, 23, 46,
   103, 116
deconstruction 154, 158
diachronic 28, 29, 113

Farrer Theory 85, 86, 98
feminism, feminist criticism 147–51, 198
form criticism 94, 99, 105–7, 108, 113, 167,
   196
Four Gospel Canon 8, 22, 74–76, 80
Four Source Theory 85, 86

gender 35, 70, 146, 147–51, 155
genre 18–20, 82, 105–7, 171, 186, 189
global readings 154–5
God 6, 13–14, 33, 36, 37, 42, 45, 49–54, 59–
   60, 65–6, 74, 77, 89, 93, 96, 106, 121, 130,
   139–40, 145, 147, 149, 152, 159, 160–1,
   166, 170–5, 191, 199
Gospel of Judas Iscariot 6
Gospel of Mary Magdalene 74
Gospel of Thomas 6, 74
Greek 2, 6, 8–9, 10, 13–14, 19, 22, 28–9, 33,
   34, 36, 51, 53, 56–72, 74, 76, 77–8, 82, 88,
   98, 104, 105, 114, 116, 120, 121, 124, 130,
   140–2, 144, 148, 194
Griesbach Hypothesis 85, 86, 98, 101

Hebrew 14, 36, 45, 51, 53, 58, 71, 82
hermeneutic of piety 167
hermeneutic of suspicion 145, 147, 167
historical criticism 28, 31, 92–111, 113–15,
   127, 152, 161, 162–3, 180, 192, 195–7
historical imagination 40–1, 92, 97
historical Jesus 40–5, 83, 87, 95, 97, 187–9
history of interpretation 168, 177

Index of Names